I Do Not Frustrate God's Grace

Carolyn P. Bynum

I Do Not Frustrate God's Grace

By: Carolyn P. Bynum, Copyright © 2017

ISBN-13 978-1-947288-18-8

ISBN-10 1-947288-18-0

All rights reserved solely by the author under international Copyright Law.. Except where designated, the author certifies that all contents are original and do not infringe upon the legal rights of any other person or work. No part of this book may be reproduced in any form without the expressed written permission of the author and publisher. The views expressed in this book are not necessarily those of the publisher.

All Scripture is taken from the authorized King James Version of the Bible.

Printed in the United States

10 9 8 7 6 5 4 3 2 1

Cover design by: Legacy Design Inc
Legacydesigninc@gmail.com

Published by: Life To Legacy, LLC
15255 S. 94th Ave, 5th Floor
Orland Park, IL 60462
877-267-7477
Life2legacybooks@att.net

CONTENTS

FOREWORD..5

ACKNOWLEDGEMENTS..6

GRACE'S SALUTATION..7

INTRODUCTION..8

CHAPTER 1 - FOCUS ON GRACE...............................11

CHAPTER 2 – GRACE REVEALS WHAT THE LAW SAYS...............20

CHAPTER 3 – GRACE TELLS THE WHOLE STORY.......................26

CHAPTER 4 – GRACE'S CALL....................................34

CHAPTER 5 – THE DYNAMIC OF GRACE.................45

CHAPTER 6 – GRACE AT THE READY.......................57

CHAPTER 7 – GRACE HAS A PARTNER CALLED TRUTH............61

CHAPTER 8 – GRACE'S UNSEEN POWER.................65

CHAPTER 9 – ONE OF GRACE'S MANY GOOD WORKS............68

CHAPTER 10 – GRACE KNOWS THE ENEMY'S LOCATION........76
AND WHAT IT MEANS

CHAPTER 11 – A CARNAL MINISTRY HINDERS GRACE............79

CHAPTER 12 – GRACE FACILITATES GOD'S PURPOSE...............90

CHAPTER 13 – DECEPTION: AN ARCHENEMY OF GRACE........95

CHAPTER 14 – GRACE CAUSES ACCUSERS TO VANISH............101

CONTENTS

CHAPTER 15 – GRACE PROVES THAT GOD REMEMBERS..........105

CHAPTER 16 – WHEN GRACE BECOMES THANKSGIVING........ 109

CHAPTER 17 – A PREPOSITION THAT CHANGED MY LIFE FOREVER..115

CHAPTER 18 – FRUSTRATING THE WORK OF GRACE................119

CHAPTER 19 – GRACE WRITES LOVE SONGS ABOUT JESUS.... 124

CHAPTER 20 – ONE OF MANY TESTIMONIES OF GRACE.......... 134

GRACE'S BENEDICTION...140

ABOUT THE AUTHOR... 141

Foreword

Galatians 1:15-16, "But when it pleased God, who separated me from my mother's womb, and called me by his grace, To reveal his <u>Son in me</u>, that I might preach him among the heathen; immediately <u>I conferred not with flesh and blood</u>."

Carolyn P. Bynum is a servant of God the Father, our Lord Jesus Christ and also my wife. She is a pastor, teacher, and songwriter of the Lord, and the best gift God could give to a man. I am proud and honored to be her husband of 41 years. We have two sons and four granddaughters.

Pastor Carolyn, as we all refer to her in Restoration Christian Ministries Center, has always served the Lord with her beautiful and anointed voice, but now with the sharing of the Gospel (Good News) for 23 years. With the Lord's anointed teaching, she has set many captives free, healed the sick, and brought knowledge to many by the Spirit of the Word, starting with me.

Pastor Carolyn has the respect of many sons of God with me being the first. She has my support in all that she does and wants to do forever. It is my pleasure and honor to serve the Lord with her in ministry.

Forever together in spirit and love,

Bishop Paul E. Bynum, Sr.

Acknowledgments

To my Beloved Jesus Christ, the Lord and the Spirit of Truth Who reveals Him to me as it pleases my Heavenly Father.

To Bishop Paul E. Bynum, Sr., my husband of over 40 years, our sons Xavier and Paul and our four grandchildren, Mileena Kathryn, Jade Alexandria, Alyssa Monet, and Elizabeth Caroline. Through each of you, I experience so much of God's love and blessings. I am among the happiest wives, mothers, and grandmothers on earth.

To my siblings, Frances, Wilma, and Richard: I am greatly enriched, loved and blessed indeed to be your sister.

To the Family at Restoration Christian Ministries, Sierra Vista, Arizona and the Body of Christ throughout the Kingdom: Walk in the Spirit, and you will receive Power to become the sons of God.

Grace, peace, love, mercy, and blessings to all.

Grace's Salutation

1 Corinthians 1:3; 2 Corinthians 1:2; Ephesians 1:2; Galatians 1:3; Philippians 1:2; Philemon 1:3 "Grace be to you and peace from God our Father, and from the Lord Jesus Christ."

1 Thessalonians 5:28 "The grace of our Lord Jesus Christ be with you. Amen."

2 Thessalonians 3:18 "The grace of our Lord Jesus Christ be with you all. Amen."

2 Thessalonians 1:2 "Grace unto you, and peace, from God our Father and the Lord Jesus Christ."

1 Peter 1:2 "Elect according to the foreknowledge of God the Father, through sanctification of the Spirit, unto obedience and sprinkling of the blood of Jesus Christ: Grace unto you, and peace, be multiplied."

2 Peter 1:2 "Grace and peace be multiplied unto you through the knowledge of God, and of Jesus our Lord."

2 John 1:3 "Grace be with you, mercy, and peace, from God the Father, and from the Lord Jesus Christ, the Son of the Father, in truth and love."

Revelation 1: 4 "... Grace be unto you, and peace, from him which is, and which was, and which is to come; and from the seven Spirits which are before his throne;"

Introduction
Vision of First Fruits

In November 2016, my husband Paul and I went on a cruise for our 40th wedding anniversary. On the third night of our cruise, I had a vision that was riveting. I do not use that word vision lightly. Since early childhood, God has graced me with visions, dreams, and keen insight. Resultantly, I have come to distinctly recognize an exigency in the message for His people in the visions.

November 2016 presented with a lot of excitement other than our happy and joyous anniversary. Notably, it featured our country's most emotionally-charged election of my lifetime. Its outcome left many people elated while many others were despondent. Despite the phenomenal effluence of emotion and resulting worldwide impact, I heard my Father's Voice loudly and clearly!

In the vision, I saw myself on the top of a very high mountain. It was so high until I must have been carried there in the Spirit for there were no physical or mechanical means to reach its summit. Everywhere I could see there was lush, ripe fruit. The fruit was at a stage where it looked almost overripe, but nothing was decaying. The fruit was much larger than we find in our markets today. God allowed me to move about freely on the mountain, but I did not see anyone else. I remember feeling a little sad because there was no one else there to partake of the abundance of fruit.

Then God allowed me to explore all around the mountain. I had a unique vantage point, and there was nothing hidden from my sight. I could see where people had settled and built homes on the sides of the mountain. Some were perched higher than others, but none was nowhere near the top. The homes were not temporary, and the people had homesteaded. From one home, I could hear music akin to the sound the wonderful people of Appalachia are known for expressing. Some people would call it "mountain music."

God used that distinct point to show me that people have settled in a place, although on a mountain, where their praise (music) is out of an experience that comes short of His glory. Please hear my heart. My comment is not a slight of any kind to those wonderful people in that region but rather a glorious example. Praise God for them because He used a part of their culture to demonstrate a spiritual truth for His Church everywhere. As if I could fly, God gave me a panoramic view of the whole mountain, and all that was happening around it. This perspective assured me that through human effort alone, there is no possible way to reach the top.

My sleep was interrupted as if gently shaken, and I knew God wanted to show me something wonderful in Christ for His people. From that moment, a precious Light has streamed into and out of my heart. The visions from God are like Scripture in that they continue to speak long after I see them.

Before our cruise ended, I had this God-inspired unction to revisit the Book of Acts and explore why the people of God allowed their joy in the Spirit to wane since God changes not. My heart began to grieve the lack of power in the Church today and go back to the beginning and see what God intended when He instituted Pentecost. When God says all things are new, that is what He means, and He does not honor our attempts to combine the old with the new. Doing so is tantamount to disobedience.

I echo the Apostle Paul to many and say, "Who has bewitched you? Who put something in place of our Beloved Lord and Savior Jesus Christ where grace abounds and caused you to build or camp short of the fullness found only in Him? Who put the mountain top off limits to you? It is accessible but only by His Spirit. Why have we allowed denominations to build and homestead on the side rather than walk in the reality of Redemption? Why are songs of defeat and death synonymous with songs of praise? Do you not know that you are alive unto God forevermore? Are you ready to come from under the spell of the Law with Its inherent self-righteousness and carnality and walk in the Power of the Spirit? If so, there is a Bounty of First-fruits of Jesus Himself waiting for you in Resurrection Power on top of Mount Zion, Heavenly Jerusalem. Grace has a Vehicle, and He is called The Resurrected Christ! You will be propelled to the very top in Him by His Spirit. Hopefully, this book will shed some of His Light that is now flooding my heart upon every reader.

Chapter One

Focus On Grace

Today, there is a lot of excitement on the "circuit" and rightly so because the Church focuses on "grace." It took a while to see the "elephant in the room," but God is right on time all the time. This glorious, fertile theme of liberty and power is echoing from hill to valley almost everywhere, but to the spiritual ear, an alarm accompanies the enthusiasm. Although grace should have always been a perpetual theme encrypted in the preaching of the Gospel of Jesus Christ, it has been and often still is entangled in too much of a mixture. "Mixture" describes the practice of preaching Law alongside grace.

Two orders are on a collision course in the Church, and the old order of religious tradition powered by the Law is now being replaced by the new order of Life in the Resurrected Christ, Jesus our Lord, powered by the Holy Spirit. A prerequisite to truly understanding the grace of God is to know that through Jesus Christ there is fulfillment and no longer a need for the Law. Otherwise, it will take much longer to eradicate the contaminated mixture and exposure that many of God's people experience in segments of today's Church.

After studying the Word one day, an image came to me in a vision. Now is a good time to tell you a little about myself. I am a Christ-centered preacher. I trust Him with my whole heart, and He shows me great and mighty things as His Word promises. I used to be concerned because I was not hearing others preach what I was preaching. Consequently, I would hold back. My thought was that certainly if God was truly speaking what I was hearing, certain notable, famous, and visible preachers would be saying it. Today, I am in awe that I was naïve enough to suppress the blessings from the Voice of the Almighty God in my concern about what people would think! Praise God for winking at my ignorance. Thank You, again and again, Heavenly Father for Your longsuffering. With that said, the following graphic may seem strange at first, but will hopefully depict the blessed lesson by the Spirit that followed when the Lord enlightened me that day.

Family, *(I call each reader "family" because we belong to One Body in Christ)*, get used to being astounded in the Lord Jesus Christ as the Spirit of Truth takes of His and shows It unto us. There are many spiritual blessings of heavenly places, but they must be seen and heard through the eyes of the Spirit. Many are now beginning to see things and say things that are "strange" to religious ears and eyes, yet to the sons of God, such things are so very refreshing to our spirits. Strange or not, they are Truth in powerful ways. Many are finding they no longer fit in the "circles" they are in, and the glorious shaking will continue until there is no longer a perceived need for it.

Now, let us view the graphic. Just allow the image to express itself to you. Ask the Holy Spirit to guide you. After all, in John 16:13,15, Jesus said, *"Howbeit when he, the Spirit of truth, is come, he will guide you into all truth: for he shall not speak of himself; but whatsoever he shall hear, that shall he speak: and he will shew you things to come. All things that the Father hath are mine: therefore, said I, that he shall take of mine, and shall shew it unto you."*

I Do Not Frustrate God's Grace

A representation of Calvary is in this graphic. Normally, two men called malefactors in Scripture are depicted hanging beside Jesus, but they have been replaced each with a table of stone which represents the Law (Two Tables of Stone). Allow me to elaborate regarding the image the Holy Spirit shared as seen in the vision described earlier. Let us go to Luke's Gospel where we find the account of the malefactors crucified with Jesus. Luke 23:32-33, 39-43 reads:

> And there were also two other, malefactors, led with him to be put to death. And when they were come to the place, which is called Calvary, there they crucified him, and the malefactors, one on the right hand, and the other on the left. And one of the malefactors which were hanged railed on him, saying, If thou be Christ, save thyself and us. But the other answering rebuked him, saying, Dost, not thou fear God, seeing thou art in the same condemnation? And we indeed justly; for we receive the due reward of our deeds: but this man hath done nothing amiss. And he said unto Jesus, Lord, remember me when thou comest into thy kingdom. And Jesus said unto him, Verily I say unto thee, To day shalt thou be with me in paradise.

Strong's Exhaustive Concordance defines a malefactor as an evil-doer, and Noah Webster defines the same as *one who commits a crime; one guilty of violating the laws, in such a manner as to subject him to public prosecution and punishment, particularly to capital punishment; a criminal.* One might ask why then is the author using two criminals to depict The Law? View these definitions through spiritual eyes along with Romans 7:7 which reads in part, "…

Nay, I had not known sin, but by the law: for I had not known lust, except the law had said, Thou shalt not covet." Thanks for the question!

In our culture, when a criminal commits a crime, he must be told what law he has broken. Without a law, there would be no reason to charge him. Without The Law, there would have been no reason for the malefactors to be doomed to death. The Innocent or Jesus was charged with the sin of the world although He was not guilty of anything. 2 Corinthians 5:21 says, *"For he hath made him to be sin for us, <u>who knew no sin</u>; that we might be made the righteousness of God in him."* Just as Jesus hanging on the Cross represents our salvation, so the malefactors who were truly guilty represent The Law, and a new dimension of our Victory in Christ is now unveiled.

Have you ever wondered why there were two of them? The two are symbolic of the Tables of Stone or the Law which was completely fulfilled the same day Jesus was crucified. If one does not see that Calvary has taken care of The Law, people will remain in a death spiral of guilt, shame, fear, and unbelief. Because of Jesus' shed Blood, believers in the Kingdom of God enter into grace or a spiritual position where Law cannot coexist. In Christ, one is not guilty, period! Because Jesus fulfilled The Law, Its glory is demolished and a Greater Glory has consumed It.

Before proceeding it is important to interject the following Scripture from Matthew 22:36-40 where a lawyer in an effort to tempt Jesus asked a question saying, *"Master, which is the great commandment in the law?"* Jesus answered, *"Thou shalt love the Lord thy God with all thy heart, and with all thy soul, and with all thy mind. This is the first and great commandment. And the second is like unto it, Thou shalt love thy neighbour as thyself. On these two commandments hang all the law and the prophets."* What powerful proof that Jesus Christ has fulfilled the Law. Also, 2 Corinthians 5:19 assures us, *that God was in Christ, reconciling the world unto himself, not imputing their trespasses unto them…"* Pure Love! Unconditional Love! Behold the majesty of the eternal Power of the Greater Glory!

It is amazing that the only Gospel, the Book of Luke, captures this aspect of The Crucifixion. Luke is the Gospel that majors on Jesus, the Man. Matthew highlights his Majesty, Mark stresses the Sacrificial Ministry of Jesus, and John focuses on His Deity. Be assured that Jesus, the Man, was identifying in every way with mankind. Although He knew no sin, Jesus was called a malefactor anyway. In response to Pilate, Jesus' accusers said, *"If he were not a malefactor, we would not have delivered him up unto thee"* (John 18:30). No one can ever honestly say that there is something the average man has to deal with that Jesus did not deal with, as well. It is interesting that Pilate went on to say, *"Take ye him, and judge him according to **your law**. The Jews therefore said unto him, It is not lawful for us to put any man to death"* (John 18:31). The problem with religious tradition then and now is that it always deals with sin in its hypocritical way, and that is why true deliverance is unknown to it.

To bring clarity in an orderly manner, let us now examine every aspect of the above Scriptures from Luke 23:32-33, 39-43 concerning the malefactors. It is important to repeat the fact that there are two of them. Two is the Bible Number for the witness and in this case, the writer is using the two malefactors as symbols of the two Tables of Stone which contained The Law. (To avoid any confusion with Bible Numbers, ten is the Bible number for Law). The point is to ensure a spiritually coherent explanation of the graphic and to leave the reader with a Spirit-sealed view that grace and law cannot abide together. Armed with such understanding, believers can navigate the freedom of redemption once for all.

Notice that these "two" were led together with Jesus to Calvary for execution. Calvary means skull. This definition is critical to the believer because it is imperative that we understand that our spiritual transformation comes by the renewing of the mind. Just think! Something eternal took place in a place called the skull. When we reflect on the battles often endured in our mind, we can easily see that God wasted no instant of infallible proof in restoring mankind unto Himself through Jesus Christ, His obedient Son. Waymarks are everywhere if one has eyes to see them! Every time we become carnally minded, remember it brings death! *"For to be carnally minded is death; but to be spiritually minded is life and peace"* (Romans 8:6).

Next, we know from Scripture that one malefactor was on the right hand of Jesus and the other on the left. No matter what direction Jesus turned His Head, He saw condemnation. He knew He was about to do away with condemnation once for all. He also knew He was obedient even to His death on the Cross and when one of the malefactors began to speak to Him reproachfully, He understood Law had done its job, and the guilty was merely lashing out. It is most profound how the Father used the other malefactor to testify that Jesus had done nothing amiss, and they instead were receiving their just reward. Even in speaking up for Jesus notice that the other malefactor (still Law) had to mention "condemnation." Let us repeat his phrase here from Luke 23:40, "Dost, not thou fear God, seeing thou art in the same condemnation?" Always consider the fact that anytime Law ministers to hearers, it has an inherent theme of condemnation no matter how eloquent, popular, defensive or simply ignorant. In this picture, both the Law and Jesus, the Lamb of God, are completing their earthly ministries.

A special note to my brethren and sisters in ministry. Every time you speak to God's people and you know they have given their lives to Him, and you minister condemnation anyway, you are not mindful that we currently have the ministry of reconciliation and God is not pleased. Be encouraged to walk in the perfect law of liberty and reflect on Romans 8:1 frequently which reads: *"There is therefore now no condemnation to them which are in Christ Jesus, who walk not after the flesh, but after the Spirit."* May I suggest majoring on The Gospel of Jesus Christ and Resurrection Life in the Spirit and the Holy Spirit will ensure you have all the Equipment necessary for your calling.

Continuing, please open your heart and hear the next point. May every minister understand thoroughly and precisely! Notice the other malefactor that testified of Jesus' innocence asked a special blessing. *"And he said unto Jesus, Lord, remember me when thou comest into thy <u>kingdom</u>"* (Luke 23:42). This malefactor, speaking to Law, asked to be remembered by Jesus when He came into His kingdom - which speaks to the government or universal dominion of God. It represents the power of supreme administration and speaks to heaven itself and the reign of Jesus, the Messiah. Now we must interject here that the Law cannot be separated-the two tables are One Law. If one goes, both have to go. Warning: a spiritual mind required! As noted in James 2:10, <u>"For whosoever shall keep the whole law, and yet offend in one point, he is guilty of all."</u> Let us follow carefully in the Scriptures how Jesus answers.

To everyone who will listen, there is greater liberating power in Jesus' response! *"And Jesus said unto him, Verily I say unto thee, Today shalt thou be with me in paradise"* (Luke 23:43). Instead of saying, *"Today shalt thou be with me in my kingdom,"* as the malefactor asked, Jesus said, *"Today shalt thou be with me in paradise."* Saints everywhere listen PLEASE! *Paradise* and My Kingdom are not the same. Paradise means a garden! It is written, *"Now in the place where he was crucified there was a garden; and in the garden a new sepulchre, wherein was never man yet laid" (John 19:41)*. When Jesus entered a place, that place changed for heaven's purpose. For instance, when He learned Lazarus was dead, He called death sleep. One must keep in mind that when referring to Him, He is inseparable from the Power of His Resurrection. Law is not allowed to reign alongside Jesus in His Kingdom. Law was fulfilled that day *in* Jesus and done away for us. Law went to a tomb in a *garden (paradise)* with Jesus that day!

By the way, do you think it happenstance in John 20:15 that Mary thought Jesus was the "gardener?" In a higher point, Jesus could have continued, "'Yes, 'Law,' today and forever you can really <u>hang out in</u> Me because you will be eternally fulfilled in Me! Because of what I am doing today, I will rise again, and one can come through Me, past the The Flaming Sword and Cherubim (Genesis 3:24) that guard the Way to the Tree of Life and live forever without worrying about whether or not he is trespassing!'" Hallelujah! In other words, Jesus was testifying, "This day, because of My obedience and through My shed Blood, Father is satisfied, and through Me, the Way to the Tree of Life is open for spiritual business!" Speaking of a garden from the book of Genesis, there is more! For some reason, man thinks Eden (the garden of God) went away, but the truth is that an eviction took place, and man left Eden. Now all can go home in Christ Jesus!

Paul told the church at Corinth, in a near desperate attempt to open their eyes: *"For if that which is done away was glorious, much more that which remaineth is glorious"* (2 Corinthians 3:11). "That" which he spoke to was the ministration of death, written and engraved in stone. *"But now we are delivered from the law, that being dead wherein we were held; that we should serve in newness of spirit, and not in the oldness of the letter"* (Romans 7:6).

"Who also hath made us able ministers of the new testament; not of the letter, but of the spirit: for the letter killeth, but the spirit giveth life" (2 Corinthians 3:6).

For the reader's edification, there are only two other places that mention "paradise" in the New Covenant. Enjoy the context! First, 2 Corinthians 12:4, *"How that he was caught up into paradise, and heard unspeakable words, which it is not lawful for a man to utter."* Allow the Ascension Life of Christ to take us fully into Himself where there are things only sons of Spirit saved by grace can utter! A son of spirit is one who is dead to self, and his life is hidden with Christ in God like the Apostle Paul told the Colossians, *"For ye are dead and your life is hid with Christ in God"* (Colossians 3:3).

The other place is Revelation 2:7, *"He that hath an ear, let him hear what the Spirit saith unto the churches; To him that overcometh will I give to eat of the tree of life, which is in the midst of the paradise of God."* Jesus is the Tree of Life! Here in Him, there is no more *"thou shalt not"* of the Law, but eat freely of the spiritual blessings in Christ. As we eat of Him, we become living letters of instruction (epistles) of Christ written on our hearts as God planned. As written in 2 Corinthians 3:3, *"Forasmuch as ye are manifestly declared to be the epistle of Christ ministered by us, written not with ink, but with the Spirit of the living God; not in tables of stone, but in fleshy tables of the heart."* This Scripture empowers us and increases our faith.

Spotlight of Grace on Law

Romans 4:13 "For the promise, that he should be the heir of the world, was not to Abraham, or to his seed, through the law, but through the righteousness of faith."

Romans 5:13 "(For until the law sin was in the world: but sin is not imputed when there is no law.)"

Romans 6:14 "For sin shall not have dominion over you: for ye are not under the law, but under grace."

Romans 9:32 "Wherefore? Because they sought it not by faith, but as it were by the works of the law. For they stumbled at that stumblingstone;"

Romans 9:33 "As it is written, Behold, I lay in Sion a stumblingstone and rock of offence: and whosoever believeth on him shall not be ashamed."

CHAPTER TWO

GRACE REVEALS WHAT THE LAW SAYS

Galatians 4: 21-31, "Now tell me, you who want to be under the Law, have you heard what the Law says? It is written that Abraham had two sons, one by the slave and the other by the free woman. The child of the slave was born in the ordinary course of nature, but the child of the free woman was born in accordance with God's promise. This can be regarded as an allegory. Here are the two agreements represented by the two women: the one from Mount Sinai bearing children into slavery, typified by Hagar (Mount Sinai being in Arabia, the land of the descendants of Ishmael, Hagar's son), and corresponding to present-day Jerusalem—for the Jews are still, spiritually speaking, "slaves". But the free woman typifies the heavenly Jerusalem, which is the mother of us all, and is spiritually "free". It is written: 'Rejoice, O barren, you who do not bear! Break forth and shout, you who do not travail! For the desolate has many more children than she who has a husband.' Now we, my brothers, are like Isaac, for we are children born "by promise". But just as in those far-off days the natural son persecuted the "spiritual" son, so it is today. Yet what is the scriptural instruction? 'Cast out the bondwoman and her son, for the son of the bondwoman shall not be heir with the son of the freewoman.' So then, my brothers, we are not to look upon ourselves as the sons of the slave woman but of the free, not sons of slavery under the Law but sons of freedom under grace."

Abraham's two sons were Ishmael and Isaac. Let us investigate the bondwoman and her son Ishmael because he was born first. With Sarah's permission as Abraham's wife, Hagar, her bondwoman, conceived Ishmael by Abraham. After Hagar had conceived, Sarah treated her harshly, and she ran away. Genesis 16:11 states that while Hagar was away, *"An angel of the LORD said unto her, Behold, thou art with child, and shalt bear a son, and shalt call his name Ishmael; because the LORD hath heard thy affliction."* The Messenger of God also told Hagar to return to her mistress. Ishmael was to be her unborn son's name which means God will hear. Interestingly, the messenger also told Hagar, "And he will be a wild man; his hand will be against every man, and every man's hand against him; and he shall dwell in the presence of all his brethren."

Here is where we need to go deeper. According to Strong's Exhaustive Concordance, "wild" means a wild ass and the sense is running wild. Ishmael, according to the Messenger of God, would be a wild man or stated differently, Adam running wild! A quick Internet search will provide some interesting facts about a wild ass. When comparing some of these facts to a carnal person's behavior or mindset, it is easy to see how one can so easily oppose Christ. A few examples will be presented, and the point will be evident very quickly.

First, a donkey is known as a burden bearer. Spiritually, this is an immediate problem because Jesus' burden is light. As written in Matthew 11:30, "For my yoke is easy, and my burden is light." A burden for a believer is equivalent to the cares of this world. The believer walking in the perfect Law of liberty in Christ has the following Scripture assimilated into his very being: *"Be careful for nothing; but in everything by prayer and supplication with thanksgiving let your requests be made known unto God"* (Philippians 4:6). A burden or weight adversely affects our ability to run well which is why Scripture cautions us to lay aside every weight, and the sin which so easily beset us. We run with patience the race that is set before us (Hebrews 12:1). One cannot be in a position of rest which Christ effected in Redemption and be burdened down at the same time.

The next example is that a wild ass will never get involved in an activity if it considers it to be unsafe. One may say this is wise, but with humans, fear can make the simplest act "unsafe." God is saying, "Fear not." Psalm 4:8 is the expression of one whom God had proven Himself again and again. David declares, *"...thou, LORD, only makest me dwell in safety."* A walk in the Spirit is a walk of faith rather than by natural sight. Where could faith possibly operate in such a mindset of a fearful feeling of being unsafe? Without faith, it is impossible to please God (Hebrews 11:6). A Spirit-led person can go where no one has gone before and do what no one has ever done in complete confidence. The key is obeying the Voice of God. The son of the promise knows that his life is governed by God's Spirit.

Another fact of the nature of the wild ass is that he has an excellent memory. If used positively, this is a great attribute. However, more often than not, memories can be painful for some. Philippians 3:13 states, *"Brethren, I count not myself to have apprehended: but this one thing I do, <u>forgetting those things which are behind,</u> and reaching forth unto those things which are before."* Many are being hindered because they hang on to the past. Too many decisions are filtered through the experiences of the past, whether good, bad, or indifferent, and the newness of Life in Christ gets smothered in the process. The lack of forgiveness is often tied to negative memories.

One last example of many more facts about the wild ass is that if he senses something wrong while traveling, he will simply not move ahead and will start digging in his heels. While this may appear as a precaution rather than stubbornness as normally ascribed, a believer should not take it as a foolproof practice. The idea emphasized here is to be Spirit-led. Many people stop and dig in along their spiritual journey because of uncertainty or leaning to their own understanding. Proverbs 3:5 discourages that practice but rather that one *to trust in the LORD with all thine heart; and lean not unto thine own understanding.* The passage continues, *"In all thy ways acknowledge him, and he shall direct thy paths."* The carnal mind wants to control itself rather than yield to the Will of God.

Spiritually, the nature of the wild ass is contrary to all that Christ speaks to yet widely accepted among many brethren. The percipient reader is now praising God because of the Biblical instance recorded in Numbers 22. The prophet Balaam and his ass give a clear picture that even an animal can be a spiritual vessel for God. 2 Peter 2:16 encapsulates the Old Testament account of God's rebuke of Balaam's iniquity by recounting, *"the dumb ass speaking with man's voice forbad the madness of the prophet."* The wild ass nature fully under the control of Almighty God! Jesus made His Triumphal Entry into Jerusalem as spoken of by the prophets to give us a picture that He has ridden out that old nature in total Victory and we can now walk or live in Him.

Returning to our opening Scripture above, notice the Apostle Paul said, Mount Sinai (where the Law was given) *typified by Hagar, Mount Sinai being in Arabia (the land of the descendants of Ishmael, Hagar's son), and corresponding to present-day Jerusalem—for the Jews are still, spiritually speaking, "slaves."* The same can be said of many churches today. Still slaves but certainly do not have to be! No matter the result of the Law is bondage, many still seem to prefer it to the freedom of holiness.

Praise the Lord for the more excellent Way and liberty in Him! Rehearsing the Scripture above, *"'But the free woman typifies the heavenly Jerusalem, which is the mother of us all, and is spiritually 'free.'"* Hebrews 12:22 confirms, *"But ye are come unto mount Sion, and unto the city of the living God, the heavenly Jerusalem, and to an innumerable company of angels..."* The Apostle Paul is imploring us as brethren to realize that we are not like Ishmael but rather like Isaac. Free indeed! Our birth is a noble one by promise! We are not sons born into slavery under the Law, and we are not to see ourselves as such. Our mother is from above, and we are free.

Another point to cement in our thinking is that *just as in those far-off days the natural son persecuted the "spiritual" son, so it is today.* We had better know it! Let us go back to Genesis and see what the son of the bondwoman, Ishmael, did to Isaac, the son of the promise. Once weaned, there was a great celebration for Isaac. Weaned from milk means ready for meat.

Hebrews 5:12 states, *"For when for the time ye ought to be teachers, ye have need that one teach you again which be the first principles of the oracles of God; and are become such as have need of milk, and not of strong meat."* Long story short, the carnal nature knows a limited number of days approach because the spirit man will no longer need milk. Why do you think carnal Christians quote so much Scripture but never walk in the Power and Light of it?

Genesis Chapter 2 reveals something paramount as a result of Isaac being weaned from his mother's milk. *"And Sarah saw the son of Hagar the Egyptian, which she had born unto Abraham, mocking"* (Genesis 21:9). Ishmael was *"mocking"* Isaac. Here is a good time to reflect on the meaning of Isaac's name. It means laughter. "Mocking" is the root meaning of "laughter." Bottom line up front, the wild nature was making sport of the new nature. Spiritually speaking, Ishmael was not using something outward but that which spoke to the essence of the new man. After all, the idea is to keep his "root" in the one whose right it is. Today it looks like this: That which should be making the new creation man laugh and rejoice or express his Kingdom experience becomes the center of amusement by the wild ass or old nature. Hear it? Hopefully.

The Apostle Paul is noted for never leaving us with the problem but the solution! I love to emulate his style. Simply, *"Cast out the bondwoman and her son, for the son of the bondwoman shall not be heir with the son of the freewoman."* As soon as Sarah noticed what Ishmael was doing in Genesis 21:10, she said, *"Cast out this bondwoman and her son: for the son of this bondwoman shall not be heir with my son, even with Isaac."* Church, Sarah is a great example and worthy of emulation. When the Church casts out the Law and fully embraces the Grace, the perfect law of liberty in Christ Jesus will enforce astonishing results.

As a reminder, the Apostle Paul addressed those who wanted to be under the Law. This chapter is also addressing the same because of the mixture in the Church today. We cannot be under the Law and grace simultaneously. Many are in bondage because of a lack of knowledge of the freedom we have as sons under grace. Paul's allegory offers great insight to the believing heart that yearns for understanding. The bondwoman and her son must never be allowed to cohabitate with the free woman and her son of the promise.

Another view spiritually is to realize this "cohabitation" attempts to take place in the mind and affects the individual and all around him. Stated another way, a carnally minded minister who ministers Law will conflict his or her audience. Individually, people will be living in a shadow that could never please God. Christ is the more excellent ministry.

Many have a tendency to look without on their pilgrimage instead of looking within. Each believer has to experience Christ personally. As we look within, spiritually speaking, the bondwoman can also picture the carnal mind or nature, and her son is the fallen man with the nature of Adam. The free woman can then symbolize the saved soul with a renewed mind, and her son is the new creation man after Christ.

Now can we begin to see the source of frustration because these two offspring can never stay in the same abode. A double mind results and the prevalent instability can now be understood in a different light. Do you agree with bondage or with freedom? *"Know ye not that ye are the temple of God, and that the Spirit of God dwelleth in you?" (1 Corinthians 3:16).* Knowledge of our true location in Christ would testify that Law with Its consequential death cannot abide there.

Spotlight of Grace on Law

Romans 4:13 "For the promise, that he should be the heir of the world, was not to Abraham, or to his seed, through the law, but through the righteousness of faith."

Romans 5:13 "(For until the law sin was in the world: but sin is not imputed when there is no law)."

Romans 6:14 "For sin shall not have dominion over you: for ye are not under the law, but under grace."

Romans 9:32 "Wherefore? Because they sought it not by faith, but as it were by the works of the law. For they stumbled at that stumblingstone;"

Romans 9:33 "As it is written, Behold, I lay in Sion a stumblingstone and rock of offence: and whosoever believeth on him shall not be ashamed."

CHAPTER THREE

GRACE TELLS THE WHOLE STORY

Matthew 12:42 "The queen of the south shall rise up in the judgment with this generation, and shall condemn it: for she came from the uttermost parts of the earth to hear the wisdom of Solomon; and, behold, a greater than Solomon [is] here."

There is a high and heavenly half that is untold in the ministering of grace. As long as the Church is busy with various programs and activities that have no eternal effect instead of being at rest, grace becomes sidelined. Grace has a full story to tell that Law prevents the hearing of her Truth. A half-truth can cause serious damage, and we are in dangerous times. When seeking a Scriptural account to magnify and simplify this great truth about to blossom, immediately the Queen of Sheba came to mind. Her experience with King Solomon is another glaring example for the Church to enter into His rest. Rest is evidence that grace is operating in fullness.

Before continuing with the resplendent picture of blessing concerning the Queen of Sheba, take note of the first mention of the word "grace" in Scripture. Genesis 6:8 reads, *"But Noah found grace in the eyes of the LORD."* Grace's essence overflows with a closer look at this verse in its context. First of all, Noah was the only man in a chaotic world, much like today, who found favor in the eyes of the LORD. Noah means rest. Grace is a one-word Spiritual System whereby a process of entering God's fullness is available. Rest is how this System functions flawlessly.

Many love to quote the 23rd Psalm which outlines how Jesus Christ,

The Great Shepherd, wants us to rest, yet they create a multiplicity of auxiliaries in His Name under the guise of "ministries of help." Mercy! On the other hand, when the Church is at rest in the Redemptive Work of the Lord Jesus Christ and Spirit-led, grace becomes an inexhaustible supply. From this seated position of rest, as the Queen of Sheba was before King Solomon, there are myriads of truths to be unfolded in Christ. Let us hear the wisdom of a greater than Solomon from His position of rest.

> And when the queen of Sheba heard of the fame of Solomon concerning the name of the LORD, she came to prove him with hard questions. 2 And she came to Jerusalem with a very great train, with camels that bare spices, and very much gold, and precious stones: and when she was come to Solomon, she communed with him of all that was in her heart. 3 And Solomon told her all her questions: there was not any thing hid from the king, which he told her not."
>
> 1 Kings 10: 1-3

Sometimes, famous ministers are known for their flamboyance, style, huge following, and the like, but this queen honed in only on Solomon's fame *concerning the name of the LORD.* What power and integrity he must have possessed! What if all we have amassed directly reflected the glory of God and honored Him? Not only consider the material substance but the ministry or operation and the citizens of the kingdom throughout the world. Solomon's majesty drew her, all her hard questions were answered, and she went out from him in fullness. Let us review the Queen's visit to the King, and by the conclusion, it will be easy to see why Jesus said she shall rise up in the judgment of a wicked, sign-seeking generation.

The Queen of Sheba had heard about the reputation, fame, glory of the Lord in relation to King Solomon. It may appear to the sensual mind that she came to impress him with *a very great train* and all the other fine things such as spices, gold, and precious stones. The fact that she came with a very great train exposes her true heart of humility. The word *train* is translated many times as *army*. It also speaks of strength, might, efficiency, and wealth. Certainly, she had no intentions of starting a conflict; therefore, her gesture most likely connotes full submission of her kingdom to the power of the Name of the LORD. She communed with Solomon of all that was in her heart, and in answering her, he did not hide anything. Christ Jesus does not want to hide anything from His people. He unveils everything by His Spirit when we commune with Him with pure hearts.

> And when the queen of Sheba had seen all Solomon's wisdom, and the house that he had built, And the meat of his table, and the sitting of his servants, and the attendance of his ministers, and their apparel, and his cupbearers, and his ascent by which he went up unto the house of the LORD; there was no more spirit in her.
> 1 Kings 10:4-5

Consider the enormous difference in *hearing* and *coming* to see. She had heard of Solomon's fame concerning the Name of the LORD and what she saw was a picture of God's glory in the earth resulting from the obedience of a servant. Wisdom took on a form that she could physically see. The result of his wisdom was so astonishing until there was no more spirit in her. The same goes for believers today as written in 1 Corinthians 1:30, *"But of him are ye in Christ Jesus, who of God is made unto us wisdom...."* There is something about Christ and His kingdom that when seen will absolutely remove one's spirit or self. Let us see why.

Next mentioned is the house Solomon had built. *"Wisdom hath builded her house, she hath hewn out her seven pillars"* (Proverbs 9:1). This queen's origin, *of Sheba*, has a dual meaning of seven or oath. Her name is unknown. Seven speaks to spiritual perfection. Could the Queen of Sheba (seven) have seen herself in the pillars of wisdom's house causing there to be *no more spirit in her?* Selah. Can the reader see yourself in Christ firmly established? *The prophet Isaiah wrote, "Hearken to me, ye that follow after righteousness, ye that seek the LORD: look unto the rock [whence] ye are hewn, and to the hole of the pit [whence] ye are digged" (Isaiah 51:1).* "Ye are God's building." (1 Corinthians 3:9). Our origin and our name become one in Him. There is no need for a separate identity because only our oneness with God matters. Concerning the oath, Christ has taken care of that too in His obedience unto Father. *"Wherein God, willing more abundantly to shew unto the heirs of promise the immutability of his counsel, confirmed [it] by an oath..."* (Hebrews 6: 17).

After the Queen of Sheba had seen all Solomon's wisdom and the house he had built, the meat of his table drew her attention. No doubt it was laden with many excellent and well-prepared choices of delicacies; however, the focus must stay spiritual. Jesus once responded when asked if he was hungry, *"My meat is to do the will of Him that sent Me and to finish His work." (John 4:34).* Once life begins in the Spirit, we must stay on course. If the *wisdom* is Christ and the *house* built by wisdom is Christ and His redeemed in Him, the meat of the king's table must be spiritual also. True sustenance for the believer is the Bread of Life, Jesus Christ. Again, Jesus said, *"I have meat to eat that ye know not of"* (John 4:32). In Christ's Revelation, to the one who overcomes is promised *hidden manna* or aspects of Him born out of intimacy and fellowship akin to the example of the Queen of Sheba.

The *sitting of his servants* probably sounds very strange to the carnal mind. Servants are expected to be up and about and waiting on others. However, here they are *sitting,* and their posture astounds the queen. Solomon's name means peace. His kingdom is a type of the kingdom of our Lord; hence the overall picture is one of rest. The word *sitting* here is translated more often habitation or dwelling. The picture is an assembly gathered to their king. This picture is also the fulfillment of the Body of Christ as a spiritual reality of the Feast of Tabernacles. Therefore, we are to gather unto our King.

The *attendance of his ministers* carries a very significant spiritual meaning for all but especially those using the title of "minister." First of all, the word attendance at its root means to stand upright, remain standing, rise, be erect, or be upright. These are not terms to be taken lightly in view of the effect ministers have on believers. Christ Jesus has wrought an eternal work in righteousness, and all those ministering to His people must flow from that Stance. The movement should always be rising upward into His Fullness. Attendance further speaks to a designated place as a member in particular of Christ's Body. Christ is able to keep us from falling yet many "ministers" continue to give occasion to the flesh. *"That is the result of a diet of the letter which kills versus the spirit which gives life"* (2 Corinthians 3:6). Otherwise one would realize he has the ability through the Spirit to minister the New Testament. We are without excuse because the ability is of God and not us.

Ministers serve. They minister unto and wait upon others. How backward this office has become in carnal church settings today! Today, many ministers seek greatness at the expense of others. Upon arrival at Capernaum one day, Jesus confronted His disciples as to why they had been disputing among themselves on the way. Of course, Jesus knew the dispute was about who should be the greatest, and their silence at His confrontation presented a teaching moment. Jesus did not rebuke them but astonished their carnal minds by saying, *"If any man desire to be first, [the same] shall be last of all, and servant of all."* (*Mark 9:35*). Internal and external disputes are also prevalent today often distracting from true ministry and resulting in works of jealousy versus works of righteousness. Remember, like the Queen of Sheba, someone is looking for the wisdom of God and His house.

What about their apparel impressed this queen? After all, could not a queen have any type of garment she desired not to mention the finest quality and style available? Their apparel was different. Remaining in spiritual thought, apparel is simply a garment that must be put on. Their apparel represents their anointing for their office. Attention all ministers! Red alert! There is nothing wrong with the wearing of vestments, but the wearing of particular external garments does not mean the minister has an anointing from God. *"But put ye on the Lord Jesus Christ, and make not provision for the flesh, to [fulfil] the lusts [thereof]"* (Romans 13:14).

Cupbearers were extraordinary people. Theirs was obviously an office that demanded much trust. They had direct access to the king. There is a connection to the cupbearer's role of providing drink to the King and sustaining life. Few cupbearers' names appear in Scripture, and Nehemiah probably comes to mind for many when the term appears in documents or mentioned in sermons. From First Kings 10, it is clear that Nehemiah's position as cupbearer gave him influence with Artaxerxes who noticed Nehemiah's sad countenance one day and gave him favor to go and repair the wall of Jerusalem. Great grace! A cupbearer's position naturally made a king take notice of him with great scrutiny. Spiritually, consider the wonderful glory of the King's Presence!

Another significant mention in Scripture of a cupbearer is the chief butler in the Pharaoh's court who was in prison, and for whom God through Joseph interpreted a dream. *Butler* is synonymous with cupbearer. In Genesis, Chapters 40 and 41, the chief butler did not face execution. He later remembered Joseph's ability of God to interpret dreams when the Pharaoh had a dream, and no one in the kingdom was able to interpret it. Of course, the phenomenal result of Joseph's subsequent ministry in that kingdom pictures Christ, the Preserver of life for His brethren and all the land. Again, the cupbearer's ministry illustrates a connection to sustaining life.

Naturally speaking, we understand the position of cupbearer, and it provides some useful information, but what is the spiritual significance of Solomon's cupbearers and their influence on the Queen of Sheba? To get to the marrow of their ministry one may just look at what was in their hand. It was a cup. A cup understandably means *to hold together*. Christ Jesus, our Lord, is The Cupbearer for all who will drink from the Fountain of Life. *"...This cup [is] the new testament in my blood, which is shed for you."* (Luke 22:20). *"...This do ye, as oft as ye drink [it], in remembrance of me." (1 Corinthians 11:25). "So, Christ was once offered to bear the sins of many; and unto them that look for him shall he appear the second time without sin unto salvation."* (Hebrews 9:28). Yet again, the Cupbearer's ministry illustrates an attachment to sustaining life and in this sense, eternal life in Christ.

Lastly, the queen saw Solomon's *"ascent by which he went up unto the house of the LORD."* After seeing all, there was *no more spirit in her*. This means that she did change forever after meeting with Solomon. Picture her getting <u>all</u> her questions answered and seeing a representation of God's kingdom in operation in the earth. Every believer could have her same experience spiritually if churches would operate in the Will of God and be led by His Spirit. The Hebrew word for *ascent* means the *whole burnt offering*. The way unto the house of the Lord is always up! In the Old Testament, Leviticus Chapter One, the *burnt offering* represented an atoning sacrifice for sin. It was a shadow of Jesus Christ our Passover. In the New Testament one finds that Ascension life in Christ. Meditate on the following verses:

> For it is not possible that the blood of bulls and of goats should take away sins. Wherefore when he cometh into the world, he saith, Sacrifice and offering thou wouldest not, but a body hast thou prepared me: In burnt offerings and sacrifices for sin thou hast had no pleasure. Then said I, Lo, I come (in the volume of

the book it is written of me,) to do thy will, O God. Above when he said, Sacrifice and offering and burnt offerings and offering for sin thou wouldest not, neither hadst pleasure therein; which are offered by the law; Then said he, Lo, I come to do thy will, O God. He taketh away the first, that he may establish the second. By the which will we are sanctified through the offering of the body of Jesus Christ once for all.

Hebrews 10:4-10

As we conclude with this beautiful example of grace in operation let us read as follows:

And she said to the king, It was a true report that I heard in mine own land of thy acts and of thy wisdom. Howbeit I believed not the words, until I came, and mine eyes had seen it: and, behold, the half was not told me: thy wisdom and prosperity exceedeth the fame which I heard. Happy are thy men, happy are these thy servants, which stand continually before thee, and that hear thy wisdom. Blessed be the LORD thy God, which delighted in thee, to set thee on the throne of Israel: because the LORD loved Israel for ever, therefore made he thee king, to do judgment and justice. And she gave the king an hundred and twenty talents of gold, and of spices very great store, and precious stones: there came no more such abundance of spices as these which the queen of Sheba gave to king Solomon.

1 Kings 10:6-10

There is vast importance in coming to see. From a spiritual perspective, in understanding, one is strategically positioned while simultaneously gaining insight into great mysteries. The eyes of faith have laser qualities. The vantage point becomes amazing in Christ. This queen learned that by coming to see, half of the truth of this kingdom had not been told. Many believers are being "powered" on the testimonies of others instead of coming to Christ and allowing Him the intimacy required to learn what is true not only of Him but also who we are in Him. Yes, wisdom is highly viewable in the Spirit! There is great blessing and happiness when one stands before the Lord continually while hearing His wisdom. God delights in His people, but many do not give Him the opportunity to express or enjoy His delight.

From the above verses, the Queen of Sheba begins to testify about the Lord as a result of seeing His wisdom and prosperity demonstrated in His people. Wake up church! God wants to show the world Christ in His people! She understood God's love for His people, and that He is a God of righteous judgment. From her own words, the queen saw that King Solomon's people acquired powerful blessings from a position of rest. It is interesting that *she gave Solomon one hundred and twenty talents of gold* which happens to serve as a reminder of the number gathered waiting on Pentecost (Acts 1:15).

One hundred and twenty! Get postured for Life in the Spirit after meeting the King. Grace for grace!

Additionally, the great store of spices and precious stones represent the sweet smell of abundant praise and thanksgiving and the glory ascribed to the King of kings. Our praise should be a reflection of His wonderful grace. Where did all the songs of defeat, sensuality, and doubt and other carnal lyrics originate? Why on earth do sons of God need to mimic worldliness? All that we have heard about our Lord is most emphatically in every sense and every realm an actual report, and that is the *rest* of the story. (Holy pun intended)!

Chapter Four

Grace's Call

God chose the natural nation of Israel to establish His holy ordinances through and to demonstrate to all other peoples of the earth what a loving, caring, protecting and above all, true God He is. In return, Israel had only to obey God's commandments and put all their trust in Him. Again, and again, the Bible records their disobedience and unbelief, causing the blessings of God to be withheld laying them bare for the enemy. Of all the nations of the earth, Israel, so *few* in light of the many, was chosen by God to do His will and good pleasure in all ways.

God's Plan from the beginning was to reconcile the whole world unto Himself, not just a select few. That is why our Lord Jesus Christ is the Lamb slain from the foundation of the world. Still today, the religious hierarchy of *"the chosen"* (not only natural Jews but all religions) seeks to usurp the rightful place of the Lord of Glory. Let one present himself as "chosen of God," and people go after "the chosen one" rather than *"the Chooser."* It does not even matter to some whether or not "the chosen one" is self-appointed. As with natural Israel, the bottom line was to produce the Son of God, so today, God's will is unchanged. Is what the huge crowd following producing sons of God, or are they merely religious tangents of self-help all in the Name of God?

This divine observation is a precursor to understanding the beauty of God's grace. Perfection's actions are stumbling blocks and offensive to imperfection. What God established in natural Israel was a type and shadow and was imperfect. All that He did externally for Israel was meant to be wrought within them and the many called ones through His Son, Jesus

Christ our Lord. The Law that ruled the chosen was no longer expected to rule them or the called when the Plan of Redemption manifested at the Cross of Christ. The Law reigning over the chosen was that of sin and death. Jesus Christ brought in a higher law called the spirit of life in Himself.

Religion (used interchangeably throughout with the religious) attempts to make law and grace coexist. That is impossible from God's perspective; however, today such mixture is perpetrated as truth. Religious people tend to believe they are "chosen" by God, and all others must come through them. They establish carnal standards, ordinances, and formalities that glorify men rather than God. Hence, anytime true grace appears, it is hated, ostracized, criticized, and much effort is expended to destroy all that it speaks to and reaches. Of course, grace speaks to Christ and just as hatred presented itself in His earthly ministry, so does it in His spiritual ministry in the earth. *"God was in Christ reconciling the world unto Himself..."* (2 Corinthians 5:19).

One of the most profound parables that exposes religion's true attitude toward God's grace is in Matthew's Gospel, Chapter 20. As you read the parable below, keep in mind that *"grace and truth came by Jesus Christ"* (John 1:17). Grace is the unmerited favor. Despite its effort, religion cannot earn grace. That is why grace is called the gift of God. We are justified freely by His grace through faith. Religion attempts to merchandize the free gift. As long as people blindly believe they must "work" for grace, there is a lot of money to be made for the religious hireling. Religion wants people to work for their justification and redemption although Christ has been made unto us all these things.

> For the kingdom of heaven is like a landowner who went out early in the morning to hire laborers for his vineyard. ² Now when he had agreed with the laborers for a denarius a day, he sent them into his vineyard. ³ And he went out about the third hour and saw others standing idle in the marketplace, ⁴ and said to them, 'You also go into the vineyard, and whatever is right I will give you.' So they went. ⁵ Again he went out about the sixth and the ninth hour, and did likewise. ⁶ And about the eleventh hour he went out and found others standing idle, and said to them, 'Why have

you been standing here idle all day?' ⁷ They said to him, 'Because no one hired us.' He said to them, 'You also go into the vineyard, and whatever is right you will received.' ⁸ "So when evening had come, the owner of the vineyard said to his steward, 'Call the laborers and give them their wages, beginning with the last to the first.' 9 And when those came who were hired about the eleventh hour, they each received a denarius. ¹⁰ But when the first came, they supposed that they would receive more; and they likewise received each a denarius. ¹¹ And when they had received it, they complained against the landowner, ¹² saying, 'These last men have worked only one hour, and you made them equal to us who have borne the burden and the heat of the day.' ¹³ But he answered one of them and said, 'Friend, I am doing you no wrong. Did you not agree with me for a denarius? ¹⁴ Take what is yours and go your way. I wish to give to this last man the same as to you. ¹⁵ Is it not lawful for me to do what I wish with my own things? Or is your eye evil because I am good?' ¹⁶ So the last will be first, and the first last. For many are called, but few chosen."

Matthew 20:1-16

While describing the kingdom of heaven, Jesus used symbols that were familiar to the disciples and the people. For example, a penny was used to symbolize the wage the laborers would receive. A penny as used here is a denarius in the Greek meaning containing ten. According to *Strong's Exhaustive Concordance*, its meaning comes from its original value of ten asses. It was a silver Roman coin and represented a day's wage. Immediately, a picture of the Law may be seen in this coin's value or the number ten.

The actual wage Jesus is speaking of in the parable above is the *fulfillment* of the value of the coin or the silver. Silver is a metal in the Bible that speaks of redemption. As a constant reminder, we are redeemed from the curse of the Law and are under grace. In getting the fulfillment of the Law, the new law of the spirit of life in Christ Jesus comes with it automatically. The only thing that could fulfill the Law was Christ Himself! Notice Jesus said the laborers subsequently hired throughout the day would receive *"whatever is right."* Although all received a penny (silver thus redemption), it was right or just. What a gift! The righteousness is in the wage. Hallelujah!

It is interesting to note that the place all were hired to work in was the householder's vineyard. The householder is the Lord of hosts. His vineyard is His chosen. Isaiah 5:7 reads in part, *"For the vineyard of the Lord of hosts is the house of Israel, and the men of Judah His pleasant plant..."* Equally as impressive is the fact that the duration of the hire is one day. Let us prepare to soar because of the unveiling of the Thoughts of the Lofty One of Israel by His Spirit.

First, we shall note the time intervals of the day at which the laborers were hired because there are astounding Scriptural parallels to see. The first workers were hired early in the morning. John 11:9 reads, *"Jesus answered, Are there not twelve hours in the day?"* In the parable, the householder wasted no time hiring laborers beginning early in the day. I am convinced from Scripture that these first laborers were the chosen few. There is absolutely nothing wrong with being chosen because the chosen are a vehicle for God's purpose. The chosen become religious when their purpose and agenda are imposed rather than God's.

The next interval is at the third hour of the day. When Pentecost was fully come, the people on whom the Holy Ghost had fallen were behaving very strangely to most at this very hour. Peter had to remind a significant number of the original chosen ones who were not in on the Experience that it was but the third hour of the day (9:00 a.m.) and those that were experiencing the Promise of the Father were not drunk as supposed. At the third hour of the day many called ones began to hear God speak directly to them in their own language from those who were unlearned in their tongue. Later, when Christ's Gospel had been preached, three thousand souls were added to the church. Oh, how these kingdom dynamics wreak havoc upon religion! A Common Denominator has reconciled Jew and Gentile and what on earth does this all mean? Religion would rather ignore it and go on with "business as usual" maintaining and guarding the Law.

At the *sixth and ninth hour*, the householder commenced employing laborers with no changes to the original plan. They too would go to the same job site with the same wage as the others. Notice these hours are placed together in the parable. All subsequent hiring after the early morning crew brought *the many called and few chosen* together with inseparable power and results. Chapter Ten of the Acts of the Apostles outlines the power of these two hours coming together regarding the Risen Christ. Read intently how the Holy Spirit merged the destiny of a devout Gentile (one of many called) with that of the Apostle Peter (one of a chosen few). Underlines are present in this book for emphasis.

Acts 10:1-48

¹There was a certain man in Caesarea called Cornelius, a centurion of the band called the <u>Italian band</u>,² A devout man, and one that feared God with all his house, which gave much alms to the people, and prayed to God alway. ³ He saw in a vision evidently about <u>the ninth hour of the day</u> an angel of God coming in to him, and saying unto him, Cornelius. ⁴ And when he looked on him, he was afraid, and said, What is it, Lord? And he said unto him, Thy prayers and thine alms are come up for a memorial before God. ⁵ And now send men to Joppa, and call for one Simon, whose surname is Peter: ⁶ He lodgeth with one Simon a tanner, whose house is by the sea side: he shall tell thee what thou oughtest to do. ⁷ And when the angel which spake unto Cornelius was departed, he called two of his household servants, and a devout soldier of them that waited on him continually; ⁸ And when he had declared all these things unto them, he sent them to Joppa. ⁹ On the morrow, as they went on their journey, and drew nigh unto the city, Peter went up upon the housetop to pray about the <u>sixth hour</u>: ¹⁰ And he became very hungry, and would have eaten: but while they made ready, he fell into a trance, ¹¹ And saw heaven opened, and a certain vessel descending upon him, as it had been a great sheet knit at the four corners, and let down to the earth: ¹² Wherein were all manner of fourfooted beasts of the earth, and wild beasts, and creeping things, and fowls of the air. ¹³ And there came a voice to him, Rise, Peter; kill, and eat. ¹⁴ But Peter said, Not so, Lord; for I have never eaten any thing that is common or unclean. ¹⁵ And the voice spake unto him again the second time, <u>What God hath cleansed, that call not thou common.</u> ¹⁶ This was done thrice: and the vessel was received up again into heaven. ¹⁷ Now while Peter doubted in himself what this vision which he had seen should mean, behold, the men which were sent from Cornelius had made enquiry for Simon's house, and stood before the gate, ¹⁸ And called,

and asked whether Simon, which was surnamed Peter, were lodged there. ¹⁹ While Peter thought on the vision, the Spirit said unto him, Behold, three men seek thee. ²⁰ Arise therefore, and get thee down, and go with them, doubting nothing: for I have sent them. ²¹ Then Peter went down to the men which were sent unto him from Cornelius; and said, Behold, I am he whom ye seek: what is the cause wherefore ye are come? ²² And they said, Cornelius the centurion, a just man, and one that feareth God, and of good report among all the nation of the Jews, was warned from God by an holy angel to send for thee into his house, and to hear words of thee. ²³ Then called he them in, and lodged them. And on the morrow Peter went away with them, and certain brethren from Joppa accompanied him. ²⁴ And the morrow after they entered into Caesarea. And Cornelius waited for them, and he had called together his kinsmen and near friends. ²⁵ And as Peter was coming in, Cornelius met him, and fell down at his feet, and worshipped him. ²⁶ But Peter took him up, saying, Stand up; I myself also am a man. ²⁷ And as he talked with him, he went in, and found many that were come together. ²⁸ And he said unto them, Ye know how that it is an unlawful thing for a man that is a Jew to keep company, or come unto one of another nation; but God hath shewed me that I should not call any man common or unclean. ²⁹ Therefore came I unto you without gainsaying, as soon as I was sent for: I ask therefore for what intent ye have sent for me? ³⁰ And Cornelius said, Four days ago I was fasting until this hour; and at the ninth hour I prayed in my house, and, behold, a man stood before me in bright clothing, ³¹ And said, Cornelius, thy prayer is heard, and thine alms are had in remembrance in the sight of God. ³² Send therefore to Joppa, and call hither Simon, whose surname is Peter; he is lodged in the house of one Simon a tanner by the sea side: who, when he cometh, shall speak unto thee. ³³ Immediately therefore I sent to thee; and thou hast well done that thou art come. Now therefore <u>are we all here present before God,</u> to hear all things that are commanded thee of God. ³⁴ Then Peter opened his mouth, and said, Of a truth I perceive that God is no respecter of persons<u>:</u> ³⁵ But in every nation, he that feareth him, and worketh righteousness, is accepted with him. ³⁶ The word which God sent unto the children of Israel, preaching peace by Jesus Christ: (he is Lord of all:) ³⁷ That word, I say, ye know, which was published throughout all Judaea, and began from Galilee, after the baptism which John preached; [38] How God anointed Jesus of Nazareth with the Holy Ghost and with power: who went about doing good, and healing all that were oppressed of the devil; for God was with him. [39] And we are witnesses of all things which he did both in the land of the Jews, and in Jerusalem; whom they slew and hanged on a tree: [40] Him God raised up the third day, and shewed him openly; [41] Not to all the people, but unto witnesses chosen before God, even to us, who did eat and drink with him after he rose from the dead. [42] And he commanded us to preach unto the people, and to testify that it is he which was ordained of God to be the Judge of quick and dead. [43] To him give all the prophets witness, that through his name whosoever believeth in him shall receive remission of sins. [44] While Peter yet spake these words, the Holy Ghost fell on all them which heard the word. [45] And they of the circumcision which believed were astonished, as many as came with Peter, because that on the Gentiles also was poured out the gift of the Holy Ghost. [46] For they heard them speak with tongues, and magnify God. Then answered Peter, [47] Can any man forbid water, that these should not be baptized, which have received the Holy Ghost as well as we? [48] And he commanded them to be baptized in the name of the Lord. Then prayed they him to tarry certain days.

Religion seeks to keep the barrier of self-righteousness solidly in place, yet it is utterly cast down and destroyed through the Power of the Gospel of Jesus Christ. It is astonishing how the many called were brought together and received the Gift of the Holy Ghost just as the few chosen. The reason lies in the simple fact *"...that God is no respecter of persons: but in every nation, he that feareth him, and worketh righteousness, is accepted with him"* (Acts 10:34). The ministry of reconciliation which is a gift will evidently set this truth forth.

We saw earlier that Jesus said there are twelve hours in the day. He is the Light of that day. The Bible records that when Jesus died on the Cross at Calvary, it became dark from the *sixth to the ninth hour*. That means from 12:00 noon until 3:00 p.m. there was total darkness. The total darkness is recorded for our learning because evil men had killed the Light of the world. Praise God for the Resurrection of our Lord! Hallelujah for His continuous Day in the life of every believer. Did you hear it?

Lastly, we come to the time interval of the day known as the *eleventh hour*. This time of day is not a reference intended by the Holy Spirit to frighten people as religion uses it to do. Instead, the eleventh-hour hiring is both herald and hallmark of God's Love for the world. The eleventh-hour corresponds with 5:00 p.m. with five being the Bible number for grace. Everything about this hour shouts of grace! The householder hired laborers with only one hour remaining in the day who would receive the same wage as those hired early in the morning. The one hour summarizes the essence of this work day. It is not about "working" at all, but rather it is all about Reward! Not only were they hired last, they got paid first! Please! What manner of Love is this?

When the early morning crew came to receive their wage, they openly murmured to the householder saying, *"These last have wrought [but] one hour, and thou hast made them equal unto us, which have borne the burden and heat of the day."* Their words contain religion's whole concept of self-importance. *"Thou hast made them equal unto us."* (Underline added for emphasis). Perhaps they are depicting the religious bewailing the loss of importance of the long robes with enlarged borders and greetings in the market? What about the chief seats in the assembly? Religion or the religious would rather make broad phylacteries (wearing Scriptures on their foreheads) instead of allowing the Holy Spirit to write the Scriptures in their hearts. Religion is not fretting over those that came at 9:00 a.m., 12 noon, or even 3:00 p.m. They simply cannot accept those that came and worked for *one hour*. This thing called grace is too much for them! Religion's true seat is in Mystery Babylon (confusion). "In *one hour*, she is made desolate!" (Revelation 18:19).

Matthew 20:13 reads, *"But he answered one of them, and said, Friend, I do thee no wrong: didst not thou agree with me for a penny?"* Love's response is so humble as indicated in the next Scripture. Greater love hath no man than this than to lay down His Life for His *friend*. Christ Himself is the wage as outlined in Romans 5:17-21.

> For if by one man's offense death reigned by one; much more they which receive abundance of grace and of the gift of righteous-

ness shall reign in life by One, Jesus Christ. Therefore, as by the offense of one judgment came upon all men to condemnation; even so by the righteousness of one the free gift came upon all men unto justification of life. For as by one man's disobedience many were made sinners, so by the obedience of one shall many be made righteous. Moreover, the law entered, that the offense might abound. But where sin abounded, grace did much more abound: That as sin hath reigned unto death, even so might grace reign through righteousness unto eternal life by Jesus Christ our Lord.

Matthew 20:16 states, *"So the last shall be first, and the first last: for many be called, but few chosen."* Whether last or first, all are Christ's. He is the *Alpha* (Beginning or First) and the *Omega* (End or Last). Many have invitations! Grace is calling! The Master calleth! Ephesians 1:4 states that *we* (Jews and Gentiles) *were chosen in Him before the foundation of the world.* All are made one in Christ. Those chosen and the called have their ground and merit in Christ alone. *"…For He is Lord of lords and King of kings and they that are with Him are <u>called</u>, and <u>chosen</u>, and <u>faithful</u>."* (Revelation 17:14).

One of the most supportive Scriptures relating to this point is captured in Ephesians 2:11-22. It reads:

> Wherefore remember, that ye [being] in time past Gentiles in the flesh, who are called Uncircumcision by that which is called the Circumcision in the flesh made by hands; that at that time ye were without Christ, being aliens from the commonwealth of Israel, and strangers from the covenants of promise, having no hope, and without God in the world: but now in Christ Jesus ye who sometimes were far off are made nigh by the blood of Christ. For he is our peace, who hath made both one, and hath broken down the middle wall of partition [between us]; having abolished in his flesh the enmity, [even] the law of commandments [contained] in ordinances; for to make in himself of twain one new man, [so] making peace; and that he might reconcile both unto God in one body by the cross, having slain the enmity thereby: and came and preached peace to you which were afar off, and to them that were nigh. For through him we both have access by one Spirit unto the

Father. Now, therefore, ye are no more strangers and foreigners, but fellow citizens with the saints, and of the household of God; and are built upon the foundation of the apostles and prophets, Jesus Christ himself being the chief corner [stone]; in whom all the building fitly framed together groweth unto an holy temple in the Lord: in whom ye also are builded together for an habitation of God through the Spirit."

Grace's Love

2 Corinthians 8:9 "For ye know the grace of our Lord Jesus Christ, that, though he was rich, yet for your sakes he became poor, that ye through his poverty might be rich."

Ephesians 1:6-7 "To the praise of the glory of his grace, wherein he hath made us accepted in the beloved. In whom we have redemption through his blood, the forgiveness of sins, according to the riches of his grace;"

1Timothy 1:14 "And the grace of our Lord was exceeding abundant with faith and love which is in Christ Jesus."

2 Thessalonians 2:16 "Now our Lord Jesus Christ himself, and God, even our Father, which hath loved us, and hath given us everlasting consolation and good hope through grace,"

Chapter Five

The Dynamic of Grace

(As seen in the life of Mordecai the Jew in the Book of Esther)

There is a clear Old Testament depiction of the ascent of the spirit man in the life of Mordecai. After Queen Vashti's dethronement, Mordecai is introduced. (If not familiar with Esther Chapter One, now is a perfect time to read it). Although the reigning king, King Ahasuerus, was a pagan king, he was of special renown with a vast kingdom and is also a type of the Lord Jesus. This chapter traces the development of the relationship between Mordecai and one of the greatest kings in history.

During a great feast, King Ahasuerus sent for his queen to display her beauty before those gathered from and throughout his kingdom, but she refused to come. Queen Vashti pictures a beautiful but disobedient church that can never reflect the glory of her king from within. Much of what is seen today in beautiful edifices filled with people outwardly adorned is actually a manifestation of Queen Vashti giving her feast and doing her own thing apart from the glory our King, the Lord Jesus Christ. Dethroned but does not realize it yet!

From another spiritual perspective, Queen Vashti represents a soul out of control with far reaching influence if not checked. The princes' response to her affront to their king as seen in Esther Chapter One is highly indicative of the leavening effect of a carnal church. Certainly, their wives and all the women throughout the kingdom would emulate her unruly behavior. Thus, she had to be dethroned. A true royal priesthood will not tolerate it and will seek a "better" queen. This quest for a new queen, who pictures the true church created for her King, is where Mordecai makes his presences known.

Mordecai's story begins in Esther 2:5-6 which reads,

Now in Shushan the palace there was a certain Jew, whose name was Mordecai, the son of Jair, the son of Shimei, the son of Kish, a Benjaminite; who had been carried away from Jerusalem with the captivity which had been carried away with Jeconiah king of Judah, whom Nebuchadnezzar the king of Babylon had carried away.

It is important that the reader observes these verses carefully as they reveal a wealth of spiritual meaning for the believer.

First, his name and lineage are noted. Mordecai means *little man*. He represents the inner man of the heart or spirit man whose hallmark is humility. He is the son of Jair whose name means he *enlightens*, and its root meaning is to become *light*. His grandfather is Shimei which means *renowned*, and his great grandfather, Kish, means *bent* as a bow. The family came from the tribe of Benjamin, the *son of the right hand*.

By now a wonderful spiritual heritage should be formed in the mind of the reader. Despite being carried away into Babylon or *confusion*, their true identity in God never changed. So, it is today! Despite all the confusion ongoing in the Church, believers have an identity in Christ that changes not. No matter what labels others place on us, the truth is that we are kings and priests unto God because of Jesus' shed Blood (Revelation 1:5-6).

Secondly, the Scriptures recorded Mordecai's location. As stated earlier, the kingdom was vast, but Mordecai is in Shushan the palace. Shushan means *lily*. The *lily* speaks to Resurrection Life. In Christ, we have the Power of His Resurrection. The king's palace was located in Shushan letting us know that we are in a kingdom with the King! It is in this place and in the knowledge of this place of life in the Spirit that the inner man or *little man* is exercised and grows up into the full measure of the stature of the Lord Jesus Christ. Note that when we are born again, our union with Christ lands us in this place of power. All that we need can present itself in this place of power because of Him. His fullness and blessings are here! We have not begun to live until we wake up to this fact. *"Ye are come unto Mount Zion"* in Christ (Hebrews 12:22). Many are always going someplace instead of embracing where we have already come in Christ in Spirit.

In Esther Chapter 2:7, Mordecai's story continues. It states, *"And he brought up Hadassah, that is, Esther, his uncle's daughter: for she had neither father nor mother, and the maid was fair and beautiful; whom Mordecai, when her father and mother were dead, took for his own daughter."* Mordecai was a steward in the overall plan of the Most High God. He is found taking care of a young maid who was *without a father or mother*. Whom do we find in the Scriptures characterized as such? Yes, Melchizedek, the Priest of the Most High God. Christ Jesus is a Priest forever after the Order of Melchizedek or the Order of an Endless Life (Hebrews 5:6). Mordecai's charge is no small one. It has an eternal reach in God. His life teaches us that as new creatures in Christ we have an infinite Power working in and through us. We are not the blueprint for quick fixes but rather for an everlasting eternity in Him. There are countless, glorious hidden mysteries yet they are wide open to the inner man of the heart.

Hadassah means *myrtle*. The Prophet Zechariah in chapter 1:8 speaks of a man on a red horse among the *myrtle trees*. It is a glorious picture of our Lord upon His Vehicle of Redemption. Also, in the Book of Nehemiah, Chapter 8, one will find the festival of the seventh month or Feast of Tabernacles restored. The command was to *"Go out into the hill country and bring back branches from olive and wild olive trees, and from myrtles, palms and shade trees, to make temporary shelters"—as it is written"* (Nehemiah 8:15). The branches came from a high place or spiritual place (hill country). As seen, the myrtle is essential in this feast of ingathering. This feast should be ongoing in the Church today, but many have not a clue of its true spiritual meaning. As we continue, the Prophet Isaiah in Chapter 55:13 states, *"Instead of the thornbush will grow the juniper, and instead of briers the myrtle will grow. This will be for the LORD's renown, for an everlasting sign, that will endure forever."* For the record, thorns and briers appeared in Genesis after the

Fall. The prophet signals to the believer that the curse is now reversed in Christ Jesus! The myrtle shows up most profoundly in things everlasting.

Hadassah was also called Esther which means *star*. Even her Persian name gave honor to God's purpose for her. When looking deeper into Esther's name, one remembers Romans 1:20 which removes every excuse for doubting God and His mighty power. Simply put, it states that one should be able to see the hidden things from the things made. We can see spiritual things by His eternal power through the things He has made in this wonderful universe. Think of a star for a moment, and let your mind go back to fifth-grade science. A star is a sphere made of gas and dust and gives off its own light. There is a powerful process going on in a star call nuclear fusion. *NASA* tells us that nuclear fusion is the energy that takes place when something goes from small to large. Nuclear fusion then is the visible act that shows us what happens within as our inner man is renewed *day by day* through the Power of the Spirit of the Living God (2 Corinthians 4:16). This should become clearer when we return to Mordecai's life.

Despite the powerful meaning of the name of Esther or *star*, she was hidden until God's purpose for her was unveiled. At no time does Mordecai try to profit from her beauty. He is never found molesting her in any form. He simply brings her up in the ways of the Lord as his very own. Mordecai was steward of a star and kept her glory pure. Oh, that the Church would have such stewards today.

God gave me a vivid dream of how one can get ahead of Him and portray a false glory. In the dream, I was facing east. East is a direction that speaks of a new day or enlightenment because the sun rises there. In light of what God is doing in my heart in this hour, I understand the dream much better now. I saw three meteors in rapid succession falling in different directions. I forgot the dream until I began to look at Esther. As stated earlier, a star gives off its own light. A meteor is often called a shooting star or falling star but is not a star at all. When a meteor enters the earth's atmosphere, it burns. The glow or streak of light signals its destruction rather than its glory. Romans 8:18 tells us, *"For I reckon that the sufferings of this present time are not worthy to be compared with the glory which shall be revealed in us."* Real stars have Christ, Who never burns out, revealed in us in every area, spirit, soul, and body. The vision of the three meteors speaks to my heart that one can fail in all these areas and burnout or remain stuck in some earthy place apart from Christ. Now is the time of His unveiling and Light to shine from within His stars!

Esther was among the virgins from whom the king was to choose his new queen. Once presented, a Dynamic that was working on Esther's behalf all along was suddenly greatly magnified. She received favor or grace from all including the king and required nothing but that which had been appointed her. Even the eunuch who was over her was named Tebeth which means *goodness*. Goodness and mercy following! Of course, Esther was the correct choice as the "better" queen! The rightful queen in her rightful place for God's purpose in and through His people.

Once crowned, there was much more to do. There is one *"Who opposeth and exalteth himself above all that is called God, or that is worshipped; so that he as God sitteth in the temple of God, shewing himself that he is God."* (2 Thessalonians 2:4). His name is Adam, the fallen man. When things seem all set, he appears until removed from our way of thinking! He showed up in Queen Esther's time as Haman. One must turn to the power of the inner man in such a time. Be reminded that Mordecai's name means little man or a type of the spirit man.

After the crowning of Queen Esther, Haman received a promotion, and Mordecai declined to reverence him. Of all Haman's wealth and power, Mordecai, who represents the inner man or spirit man, refused to bow down to him. Haman went to such lengths as to offer his own silver for the destruction of the Jews. He complained to the king that certain people were in the land whose laws were diverse from all people (Esther 3:8). He stopped at nothing until the decree of destruction went out.

Slowing down a bit for a spiritual breath, notice Haman's offer of silver. Silver is a metal in Scripture that speaks to redemption. Notice how the Adamic nature always works to counter the spirit man's effort and growth.

For example, the believer attempts to pray, and his mind is full of rapid carnal thoughts that seem relevant only during times of prayer and meditation. Further, Haman erected gallows of 50 cubits. Fifty denotes Pentecost or the infilling of the Holy Ghost. The dimensions are divinely inspired to show not only that Adam does not want the believer to understand His redemption in Christ but the Spirit's Power either. Here we have Haman in a nutshell. He is pulling out all stops to thwart the believer's growth in Christ absolutely. His real target is always the Seed or Christ Jesus.

When the decree went out to kill the Jews, Mordecai immediately called for a time of fasting and mourning for all the Jews. Esther was not aware of Haman's plot but learned that Mordecai was in sackcloth and ashes. When she discovered his state, she sent him clothing, but he refused.

Although Mordecai mourned outwardly, as a representative inner man, he could receive "covering" from one Source only. Mordecai sent a copy of the decree to Esther along with a declaration of certainty of God's deliverance whether by Esther or not. He further informed her that if she did not intercede, she and her father's house would be destroyed.

Despite her fear of approaching the king without being summoned, Esther boldly decided to make a move. She stated,

> Go, gather together all the Jews that are present in Shushan, and fast ye for me, and neither eat nor drink three days, night or day: I also and my maidens will fast likewise; and so will I go in unto the king, which is not according to the law: and if I perish, I perish.
> Esther 4:16

All flesh has to be under subjection in such a spiritual situation. Mordecai did all Esther commanded. In sync with a saved soul, which Esther now represents, the spirit man or inner man can go forth in power in the earth. Not by and by but presently. Together, Esther and Mordecai now reflect a believer with no schism within whose heart and mind are one in Christ. The nuclear fusion spoken of earlier, though powerful it may be, pales in comparison to the Power of God that is working in and through them at this point.

Third day! After three days of fasting, the queen went in her royal apparel to visit her king. Fear vanishes in this kind of faith. Again, the great

Grace Dynamic is in force. Esther did not begin by ranting or crying to the king about Haman or his plot but instead by entreating him. The Spirit giving her what to speak in that hour offered to host a banquet for the king and Haman. Spiritual sight knows that a banquet would require drinking of wine or "spiritually speaking," the flowing of the Spirit in the face of the enemy. The king obliged her. Pause and think for a moment. How did Esther acquire the favor of the king? Simply by being a star with the king's glory radiating from within her and with her royal apparel upon her. May we all learn what it means to be instead of worrying about what we need to do in Christ.

The King could not sleep. Divine intervention! Of all the things, a sleepless night could bring, the king wanted his chronicles and therein was his hap to fall upon what Mordecai, the little man, had done to preserve the king's life. A great deed recorded in time that received no recognition. Believers are often in this mode. I personally refer to it as being in sacrifice mode. There are times when it seems that our lives are for the benefit of others and little thanks ever mentioned. Just remember Jesus in such times and keep serving. Do not worry; the King has a record and a reward! King Ahasuerus was urgent in the matter of ensuring proper recognition for such a courageous act and wanted to know who was present at court. Guess who entered on the Divine queue? Haman! When asked how to reward such a man, Haman poured it on thinking all the while it was for himself. The fallen man always seeks glory he was never meant to have. The reward of the true King is never for the fallen man but rather the spirit man.

After devising a glorious plan of reward intended for himself, Haman had to lead Mordecai, the little man, through the city on a horse, dressed in the king's robe and wearing a crown. Eternal life Power in full operation and on display for all to see. Haman had to decree, *"Thus shall it be done unto the man whom the king delighteth to honour"* (Esther 6:7). Jesus Christ, the Resurrection and the Life must be on full display in His believer!

Queen Esther gave her banquet and revealed the wickedness of Haman. *"So they hanged Haman on the gallows that he had prepared for Mordecai. Then was the king's wrath pacified"* (Esther 7:10). The king gave all of Haman's house to Esther, the queen. The king received a revelation regarding Mordecai's relationship to Esther. Notice that the relationship between Queen Esther and Mordecai had a particular time to be revealed. There is no need to push, "network," or jockey for a position in the Kingdom. God has a plan for all.

Esther then placed Mordecai over Haman's house, and the king gave Mordecai a ring he had given Haman. Examine the picture drawn by these facts. Esther, who portrays the Church or the saved soul, is given all Haman's house. Stated another way, the Church or the saved soul received all the fallen man's property. That is his dominion, power, and belongings. Our inner man or *"spirit is joined to the Lord as One Spirit"* as found in 1 Corinthians 6:17. The residue of the carnal man's "estate" is lodged in the mind (soul realm) that has not entirely put on Christ; therefore, the spirit man must be in control of the carnal man's "estate" in the life of every believer until full maturity in Christ.

Now we see the Spirit's reason for Esther placing Mordecai or the spirit man over Haman's estate as manager. The fallen man's property is temporal, and since his removal from the scenario, the relationship between Queen Esther, Mordecai and the king speak to an eternal one. Anything temporal must be under the full control of the spirit man as represented by Mordecai. He now has the king's ring! Never forget that three times in the Book of Esther the king offered his queen "even to the half of the kingdom." See how insignificant Haman's estate becomes when compared to half of the kingdom! When believers truly embrace this spiritual fact, the great quest for temporal blessings will cease. The Scriptures state, *"Seek ye first the kingdom of God and His righteousness and all these things will be added unto you"* (Matthew 6:33).

Assurance of full salvation from our enemy is critical for powerful ministry. In Esther Chapter 8, the queen implored the king to counteract the evil of Haman. Although Haman is dead physically, his acts are still alive. The Queen's request recorded in Esther 8:5:

> If it pleases the king, and if I have found favor in his sight and the thing seems right to the king and I am pleasing in his eyes, let it be written to revoke the letters devised by Haman, the son of Hammedatha the Agagite, which he wrote to annihilate the Jews

who are in all the king's provinces. For how can I endure to see the evil that will come to my people? Or how can I endure to see the destruction of my countrymen?

The king not only responded to his queen with a profound answer but to Mordecai also. The king restated the fact that he had given Haman's house to his queen and hanged him. In other words, Church, this pictures Christ Jesus Who has taken out our enemy on His Cross and given us a work of faith to do as well. The king charged Esther and Mordecai, <u>"You yourselves write a decree concerning the Jews, as you please, in the king's name, and seal it with the king's signet ring; for whatever is written in the king's name and sealed with the king's signet ring no one can revoke"</u> (Emphasis mine). We must use the authority Christ Jesus gave us! Is it now time for a priesthood to do greater works that our High Priest, The Lord Jesus, said we should!

As soon as Mordecai engaged in his authority in obedience to the king, he went out from the king's presence in spiritual or heavenly array, and Shushan or the place of eternal life power rejoiced and was glad. Heaven rejoiced! Esther 8:16-17 reads:

> The Jews had light and gladness, joy and honor. And in every province and city, wherever the king's command and decree came, the Jews had joy and gladness, a feast and a holiday. Then many of the people of the land became Jews, because fear of the Jews fell upon them.

What a glorious formula, Church! As Mordecai, we have been arrayed in special apparel as well when we put on the Lord Jesus Christ. Now simply walk in the Spirit; obey Christ Jesus our King; exact the power He has given us; allow His Presence within us to bring light, joy, and gladness to others; celebrate His goodness, and observe His reverential fear fall upon all who will then want to become one with Him!

On the very day the enemies of the Jews had hoped to overtake them, the opposite occurred, and the Jews overpowered those who hated them. All officials throughout the king's realm helped the Jews. They knew Mordecai was great in the king's palace, and his fame had spread throughout all the provinces. Mordecai's prominence increased. The inner man was being strengthened with might! The Jews defeated all their enemies *with the stroke of the sword*. In other words, the sword speaks to the Word of God which will destroy every enemy of the believer.

Of all the enemies destroyed, noteworthy is the fact that the *ten sons of Haman* were hanged on gallows as their father was. The number ten speaks to Law. Law and grace cannot exist together. 2 Corinthians 3:6 tells us that God has made us able ministers of the New Testament; not of the letter, but of the spirit: for the letter killeth, but the spirit giveth life.

The life in Christ and the authority given us often appear distorted because the Law lingers over the heads of many. The Adamic nature enjoys this ignorance and maintains a foothold where he has absolutely no authority. Remember that through Christ we have the same testimony of Esther 9:5 which reads, *"Thus the Jews defeated all their enemies with the stroke of the sword, with slaughter and destruction, and did what they pleased with those who hated them."* Remembering so great a deliverance, Mordecai and Queen Esther established a two-day celebration called the Feast of Purim, commemorated to this day. The inevitable result of such a time of peace and truth is feasting, joy, and gladness! The Kingdom has come!

Many notice that God's Name does not appear in the Book of Esther. Even so, there is no doubt that His providence and protection are in full force on behalf of His people. Could it be that this God-inspired Book is guiding people of faith in a new and living way by the Spirit? God is a Spirit (John 4:24). Though not named, His Evidence is everywhere! The name connotes nature, especially in the Scriptures.

It is this writer's belief that God is seeking a people who will live in the Spirit and walk in the Spirit (Galatians 5:25), bearing His Nature. No specific name for Him is needed because His Essence in fullness and purity flows through people! It could be none other than Himself!

Prayerfully, this chapter helped put light on the role, power, and ascent of the spirit man and his relationship and work in the restoration of the soul and ultimately the Church. The Book of Esther ends with emphasis on the greatness of Mordecai or the *little man*. Within the chronicles of the kings of Media and Persia it is written of Mordecai's greatness to which a great king advanced him. Mordecai the Jew was second only to this great king. As with Mordecai and the king during his time, so should the spirit man or inner man of the heart of every believer be to the Lord Jesus Christ.

Drawing a further analogy, just as Mordecai was great among all the Jews and well received by the multitude of his brethren, so should it be among believers close at heart and joined to the Lord as one Spirit. Finally, of Mordecai, the Bible adds that he sought the good of his people and spoke peace to all his countrymen. May God bless our lives so that we may bless each other in the same manner as Mordecai.

Grace's Warning

Ephesians 4:29 "Let no corrupt communication proceed out of your mouth, but that which is good to the use of edifying, that it may minister grace unto the hearers."

Hebrews 13:9 "Be not carried about with divers and strange doctrines. For it is a good thing that the heart be established with grace; not with meats, which have not profited them that have been occupied therein."

1 Peter 5:5 "Likewise, ye younger, submit yourselves unto the elder. Yea, all of you be subject one to another, and be clothed with humility: for God resisteth the proud, and giveth grace to the humble."

James 4:6 "But he giveth more grace. Wherefore he saith, God resisteth the proud, but giveth grace unto the humble."

Jude 1:4 "For there are certain men crept in unawares, who were before of old ordained to this condemnation, ungodly men, turning the grace of our God into lasciviousness, and denying the only Lord God, and our Lord Jesus Christ."

Chapter Six

Grace at the Ready

Saul of Tarsus was on his way to persecute the Church of the Lord Jesus Christ. While on the road to Damascus, he experienced a life changing transformation. That radical change is due to none other than THE Resurrected Christ. He is the True Light of the world, the Sun of Righteousness with healing in His Wings, brighter than the noonday! Saul met the Christ!

Let us explore the surroundings of Saul at that moment before going on. He was on his way to Damascus, a place which means silent is the sackcloth weaver. Those familiar with the use of sackcloth worn in the Bible may recall its association with mourning or humiliation. Saul and the Old Order that he speaks to was passing fast. Acts Chapter 9 provides the full details of the meeting with the Lord. There one will find a question posed to Saul by the Lord. *"…Saul, Saul why persecutes thou Me?"* (Acts 9:4). Persecution is one of those loaded terms requiring several ways to unveil its meaning. It means to pursue (in a hostile manner), *to make to run or flee, put to flight, drive away, in any way whatever to harass, jeer or deride, trouble, molest one.* One man was causing all this havoc to the Body of Christ.

The reader will find that persecution is synonymous with the Old Testament term for *"mocking"* as Ishmael, the son of the bondwoman did to Isaac, the son of the promise (Genesis 21:9). *Mocking* is the root meaning of *laughter*. Laughter is the meaning of Isaac's name. However, it is most noteworthy that the term *mocking* has a root meaning of *chasm* which is found only once in Scripture in Luke 16:26 of *a great gulf fixed.* The two, representing law and grace, were never meant to be together.

Saul encountered the Christ and fell to the earth as dead. This act was identifying with his state apart from Christ. The Voice of this same Christ must speak volumes on our earth today! The flesh or earthy man must hear His Voice. Christ Jesus is Light, and His Light will shine in every area of our lives.

John 1:4 "In him was life, and the life was the <u>light</u> of men."

John 8:12 "Then spake Jesus again unto them, saying, I am the <u>light</u> of the world: he that followeth me shall not walk in darkness, but shall have the light of life."

John 9:5 "As long as I am in the world, I am the <u>light</u> of the world."

After proclaiming Himself as the One Saul was persecuting, Jesus told him simply, *"It is hard for thee to kick against the pricks"* (Acts 9:5). To do so is to offer vain and perilous or ruinous resistance. Next, is seen a snapshot of death to self in progress. Saul could not see, eat or drink for three days! The world was cut off, and Resurrection Life could commence. Grace is then at the ready! Ananias which means *"whom Jehovah has graciously given,"* represents grace and is commissioned by the Spirit to go to Straight Street to the house of Judas (praise) where Paul prayed.

Paul sovereignly landed on a way or street that means *straight forward, upright, true, sincere*. Notice how "grace" answered the Spirit. Acts 9:10 reads, *"There was a certain disciple at Damascus, named Ananias; and to him said the Lord in a vision, Ananias. <u>And he said, Behold, I am here, Lord.</u>"* The discipline of grace is seen clearly in Acts 9:10-18. Grace answers to the Christ! The way ordained for grace is *via* "Straight Street." It is a straight forward, upright, genuine and sincere way. The Way is Jesus Himself Who said in the Book of John 14:6, *"...I am the way, the truth, and the life: no man cometh unto the Father, but by me."* The reader may delve deeper by reading Isaiah Chapter 35 concerning the Way that Jesus is.

Ananias or *grace* obeyed and went to the house of Judas or praise. Grace was working on both ends because Saul saw Ananias or grace coming in a vision. Be confident that grace knows all about what one has done but does not judge. Notice Acts 9:13-14 where Ananias is speaking: *"Then Ananias answered, Lord, I have heard by many of this man, how much evil he hath done to thy saints at Jerusalem: And here he hath authority from the chief priests to bind all that call on thy name."* Nevertheless, he obeyed the Lord and did as commanded without judging because we have already been judged in Christ. Always remember that all things are under subjection to Jesus Christ! (Acts 9:13-16 with Hebrews 2:8-9).

Grace calls us, "Brother!" Wonderful Jesus! Acts 9:17 states,

> And Ananias went his way, and entered into the house; and putting his hands on him said, Brother Saul, the Lord, even Jesus, that appeared unto thee in the way as thou camest, hath sent me, that thou mightest receive thy sight, and be filled with the Holy Ghost.

Did you notice from this verse that grace already knows what happened in the encounter with Jesus? See how grace also knows that a "chosen vessel" needs to be filled with the Holy Ghost to do the Master's will. Grace acts as an agent facilitating the infilling of the Holy Ghost with immediate results. The anointed results of the apostolic ministry of GRACE is that scales fell from Saul's eyes and he received his sight. He arose (an outward act of his inward resurrection) and was baptized. All this was done, and he then received meat and strength, and straightway he preached Christ that He is the Son of God. Flesh and blood will not show anyone that!

Grace's Salvation

Romans 3:24 "Being justified freely by his grace through the redemption that is in Christ Jesus:"

Romans 11:6 "And if by grace, then is it no more of works: otherwise grace is no more grace. But if it be of works, then is it no more grace: otherwise work is no more work."

1 Corinthians 1:4 "I thank my God always on your behalf, for the grace of God which is given you by Jesus Christ;"

Ephesians 2: 5 "Even when we were dead in sins, hath quickened us together with Christ, (by grace ye are saved;)"

Ephesians 2: 8 "For by grace are ye saved through faith; and that not of yourselves: it is the gift of God:"

Hebrews 2:9 "But we see Jesus, who was made a little lower than the angels for the suffering of death, crowned with glory and honour; that he by the grace of God should taste death for every man."

Titus 2:11 "For the grace of God that bringeth salvation hath appeared to all men,"

Titus 3:7 "That being justified by his grace, we should be made heirs according to the hope of eternal life."

Chapter Seven

Grace has a Partner Called Truth

"For the law was given by Moses, but grace and truth came by Jesus Christ" (John 1:17).

While majoring on God's grace, do not forget about the accompanying "truth" that came along with it by Jesus Christ. "Truth" is the Person, Jesus Christ the Righteous! He said, *"I am the way, the truth, and the life: no man cometh unto the Father, but by me."* (John 14:6). To the hearing ear, part of the problem with today's ministry on grace in some cases is the fact that the Truth is missing His rightful place. Many want the benefits of grace while maintaining their carnal appetites. This practice will not help one gain any spiritual ground.

There is a drill in the military called *"Mark time, March!"* During this particular exercise soldiers march in place without any forward movement. The feet move up and down in mechanical precision, but the body of soldiers stays in the same position. With one drill, a microcosm of the most powerful natural fighting force on earth is temporarily put on hold, so to speak. The adversary uses this "drill" in many churches whenever he gets ready, and the people simply march in place instead of moving onward and upward in the ways of the Spirit. How does he get a foothold? Many live in the flesh instead of the Spirit. Grace becomes a Christ-calibrated instrument of righteousness when exercised in a Spirit-filled life. The life of the believer is an ascension life, and Christ Jesus did not redeem us to stay in one position simply going through the motion of "walking in the Spirit." "Let us go on unto perfection"(Hebrews 6:1).

According to 2 Corinthians 3:7, the Apostle Paul told the Church at Corinth,

> But if the ministration of death, written and engraved on stones, was glorious so that the children of Israel could not steadfastly behold the face of Moses for the glory of his countenance; which glory was to be done away:

There is a glory that many hold on to today that has been done away in the Cross of Christ. When we minister "thou shalt not" instead of "blessed are," we put that which is more excellent in abeyance. Truth be told, the enemy of righteousness does not care how much is preached about grace as long as the truth of Christ is never included. According to Ephesians 1:3, *"God has blessed us with all spiritual blessings in heavenly places in Christ."* Believers should hear about these blessings of heavenly places in Christ instead of condemnation. Romans 8:1 assures, *"There is therefore now no condemnation to them which are in Christ Jesus, who walk not after the flesh, but after the Spirit."* The focus should be on the ministry of the Spirit. He will ensure grace ministers to the hearer, so one will not be inclined to walk after the flesh. Grace through Spiritual ministry negates Law in every way.

The focus verse above follows a wondrous verse, John 1:14 which says, *"And the Word was made flesh, and dwelt among us, (and we beheld his glory, the glory as of the only begotten of the Father,) full of grace and truth."* The shortcoming for many is the lack of understanding that Jesus was the Word made flesh. Let that soak in a moment. The Word of God is the only thing exalted above His Precious Holy Name (Psalm 138:2). As such, Jesus was full of grace and truth!

A careful listen today will find a deficit of the Word ministered wherein lies a big problem for the believer. The Spirit of the Word is what gives life and gives grace unlimited opportunity to be appropriated. Man's self-help quips may last for a little while, but they will never sustain the believer. Pseudo is not Truth! Too many accept the deficit as the actual grace of God. A few trinkets and other toys are not the expected end of God's grace. Like a thermostat, the setting of our hearts must be on things eternal versus temporal. Relegating God's enormous grace to mundane things is beggarly indeed.

There are terms in Scripture concerning truth that should get our attention in light of what most people seem to be experiencing today. A few examples include Jesus declaring, *"I am the true vine"* (John 15:1). It is fair then to believe that a fraud exists. There is a fraud perpetrating to be the Substance of God. A vine carries all the substance to the fruit and obviously, some people are getting their spiritual nourishment from another source. There are innumerable distinctions between Jesus and false prophets yet multitudes keep getting duped meeting after meeting.

Another example that keeps me upright is in the Book of Ephesians 4:24, *"And that ye put on the new man, which after God is created in righteousness and true holiness."* Someone may think true holiness means a particular dress code or certain mannerisms that have absolutely nothing to do with holiness at all. Vestments or other items of distinction are not synonymous with true holiness. True holiness is a spiritual state of being. God did not say do holy, but rather, *"Be ye holy for I am holy"* (1 Peter 1:16). Anything outward is doing. After all, a clown wears distinct clothing. If a moth can corrupt it, it is not the true! As Jesus cautioned, *"Lay up for yourselves treasures in heaven, where neither moth nor rust doth corrupt..."* (Matthew 6:20).

Further, Hebrews 8:2 reads, *"A minister of the sanctuary, and of the true tabernacle, which the Lord pitched, and not man."* Many spend decades using resources, energy, and aspirations for a beautiful physical church to worship and fellowship. That is a great feat in itself but not when the people see a physical structure as the tabernacle of God. The true tabernacle is Christ, and His Church makes up His Body. How many members really know what Hebrews 3:6 says? To refresh it states, *"But Christ as a son over his own house; whose house are we, if we hold fast the confidence and the rejoicing of the hope firm unto the end."*

Many understand that such examples can fill an entire book. However, let us consider another. Scripture states in 1 John 2:8, *"Again, a new commandment I write unto you, which thing is true in him and in you: because the darkness is past, and the true light now shineth."* Something powerful is true in every believer right now. Focusing on the Redemptive Work of Jesus Christ through His Holy Spirit will unveil this truth in and to the believing heart. In faith, one will find that all the things requested of God are already answered because of His Son. That is why He is called Faithful and True (Revelation 19:11). Grace has an awesome Partner, and He is called Truth!

Grace's Ministry

Romans 5: 15 "But not as the offence, so also is the free gift. For if through the offence of one many be dead, much more the grace of God, and the gift by grace, which is by one man, Jesus Christ, hath abounded unto many."

Romans 5: 17 "For if by one man's offence death reigned by one; much more they which receive abundance of grace and of the gift of righteousness shall reign in life by one, Jesus Christ."

Romans 5: 20-21 "Moreover the law entered, that the offence might abound. But where sin abounded, grace did much more abound: That as sin hath reigned unto death, even so might grace reign through righteousness unto eternal life by Jesus Christ our Lord."

Ephesians 3: 7-8 "Whereof I was made a minister, according to the gift of the grace of God given unto me by the effectual working of his power. Unto me, who am less than the least of all saints, is this grace given, that I should preach among the Gentiles the unsearchable riches of Christ;"

1 Peter 4:10 "As every man hath received the gift, even so minister the same one to another, as good stewards of the manifold grace of God."

1 Peter 5: 10 "But the God of all grace, who hath called us unto his eternal glory by Christ Jesus, after that ye have suffered a while, make you perfect, stablish, strengthen, settle you."

CHAPTER EIGHT

GRACE'S UNSEEN POWER

(As seen in *On*, The Son of Peleth)

Scripture Reading:

Now Korah the son of Izhar, the son of Kohath, the son of Levi, with Dathan and Abiram the sons of Eliab, and On the son of Peleth, sons of Reuben, took men; and they rose up before Moses with some of the children of Israel, two hundred and fifty leaders of the congregation, representatives of the congregation, men of renown. They gathered together against Moses and Aaron...

Numbers 16: 1-3

On was one of those who took part in the rebellion of Korah never the less not mentioned in the resulting judgment. The name *"On"* means *wealth or vigor*. A further meaning is to attempt something and be successful at it. However, the spiritual power for this short lesson is at the base meaning of his name which is to pant or cry out. Psalm 42 is a psalm for the Sons of Korah, and it begins, *"As the deer pants for the water brooks, so pants my soul for You, O God."* At some point On was able to see that observing the lying vanity of rebellion was to forsake the mercy of God. There is no record of On's repentance, yet as the base meaning of his name suggests, somewhere he panted or cried out to God for mercy and *"where sin abounded, grace did much more abound"* (Romans 5:20).

On is a character through whom the love, grace, and mercy of God are on full display. As with any believer whose soul pants for or cries out to God with creation's groan, God hears and delivers. *On* is not heard of anymore because he pictures one becoming one with God. The whole point of the panting soul is to go on to maturity in Christ leaving all the interests of self behind. As seen in Numbers 16:2, *On* was descendent of Reuben. The Holy Spirit inspired that fact to be recorded for our learning. Reuben's name means behold a son. *On* is a further picture of a believer who is saved by grace through faith and becomes an heir whose life is hidden with Christ in God.

Grace's Power

Acts 20:24 "But none of these things move me, neither count I my life dear unto myself, so that I might finish my course with joy, and the ministry, which I have received of the Lord Jesus, to testify the gospel of the grace of God."

Acts 20:32 "And now, brethren, I commend you to God, and to the word of his grace, which is able to build you up, and to give you an inheritance among all them which are sanctified."

Romans 6:1-2 "What shall we say then? Shall we continue in sin, that grace may abound? God forbid. How shall we, that are dead to sin, live any longer therein?"

Romans 6:14 "For sin shall not have dominion over you: for ye are not under the law, but under grace."

Romans 6:15 "What then? shall we sin, because we are not under the law, but under grace? God forbid."

Romans 16:20 "And the God of peace shall bruise Satan under your feet shortly. The grace of our Lord Jesus Christ be with you. Amen."

2 Corinthians 9:8 "And God is able to make all grace abound toward you; that ye, always having all sufficiency in all things, may abound to every good work:"

2 Corinthians 12: 9 "And he said unto me, My grace is sufficient for thee: for my strength is made perfect in weakness. Most gladly therefore will I rather glory in my infirmities, that the power of Christ may rest upon me."

Ephesians 2:7 "That in the ages to come he might shew the exceeding riches of his grace in his kindness toward us through Christ Jesus."

Hebrews 12:28 "Wherefore we receiving a kingdom which cannot be moved, let us have grace, whereby we may serve God acceptably with reverence and godly fear:"

Chapter Nine

One of Grace's Many Good Works

(As seen in the account of the Good Samaritan)

Scripture Reading: Luke 10: 25-37

^{25}"And, behold, a certain lawyer stood up, and tempted him, saying, Master, what shall I do to inherit eternal life? ^{26} He said unto him, What is written in the law? how readest thou? ^{27} And he answering said, Thou shalt love the Lord thy God with all thy heart, and with all thy soul, and with all thy strength, and with all thy mind; and thy neighbour as thyself. ^{28} And he said unto him, Thou hast answered right: this do, and thou shalt live. ^{29} But he, willing to justify himself, said unto Jesus, And who is my neighbour? ^{30} And Jesus answering said, A certain man went down from Jerusalem to Jericho, and fell among thieves, which stripped him of his raiment, and wounded him, and departed, leaving him half dead. ^{31} <u>And by chance there came down a certain priest that way: and when he saw him, he passed by on the other side.</u> ^{32} And likewise a Levite, when he was at the place, came and looked on him, and passed by on the other side. ^{33} But a certain Samaritan, as he journeyed, came where he was: and when he saw him, he had compassion on him, ^{34} And went to him, and bound up his wounds, pouring in oil and wine, and set him on his own beast, and brought him to an inn, and took care of him. ^{35} And on the morrow when he departed, he took out two pence, and gave them to the host, and said unto him, Take care of him; and whatsoever thou spendest more, when I come again, I will repay thee. ^{36} Which now of these three, thinkest thou, was neighbour unto him that fell among the thieves? ^{37} And he said, He that shewed mercy on him. Then said Jesus unto him, Go, and do thou likewise."

The above Scripture provides insight into a crippling problem in most of the Church today. It begins with a dialog between a particular lawyer and Jesus, the Living Word of God. A lawyer was one well acquainted with, skilled in, and experienced in the Law. Romans 8:3 reads, *"For what the law could not do, in that it was weak through the flesh, God sending his own Son in the likeness of sinful flesh, and for sin, condemned sin in the flesh."* The picture before the reader then is a passing order (Law) confronted with the New (Christ), yet the passing order attempts to continue to *justify* itself! Oh, the self-righteousness of the religious system! The New Order is by the Spirit of God, and 2 Corinthians 3:6 informs us that Christ Jesus has made us able ministers of the New Testament, *"not of the letter, but of the spirit: for the letter killeth, but the spirit giveth life."* The lawyer sought to justify himself or make himself righteous by asking Jesus, *"And who is my neighbour?"* This question presented a compelling opportunity for the Master to teach and provide a glimpse into all that He would accomplish in His Work of Redemption.

Unlike the particular lawyer in the above Scripture who sought to justify himself, believers must realize and fully embrace the fact that Jesus, *"... is made unto us wisdom, righteousness, sanctification and redemption"* (1 Corinthians 1:30). Our belief is strengthened as we learn more about Christ. The lawyer asked Jesus, *"And who is my neighbour?"* That simple question gauged him precisely and is a powerful teaching point for all as will become evident in the parable of Jesus concerning the certain Samaritan.

Verse 30 above sets the stage for Jesus' response to the lawyer. *"And Jesus answering said..."* The Greek word "answering" literally means *to take up in order to raise, to bear on high.* Spiritually, Jesus took him up or stated another way, removed the ground from under him simply by responding. Hallelujah! Higher ground! This lawyer, of course, represents the Law. Jesus did not deal with Law on its own territory; He fulfilled It. This lawyer probably understood that in the Jewish culture, a neighbor meant any Hebrew member of their nation which is also probably why he thought he could justify himself with the question. However, Jesus brought the lawyer to the all-conquering ground of Eternal Spirit which brings every nation, kindred, and tongue together in Himself. The lawyer was familiar with a priest and a Levite but bringing a Samaritan into the picture made the situation quite uneasy for him. After all, he would have had no dealings except with the Jews. Even the woman at the well (John 4:9) reminded Jesus that *"the Jews had no dealings with the Samaritans."* Jesus came removing partitions, and flesh prevented Law from doing the same.

In the verses above, the terrible plight of a victim referred to *as a certain man* is before us. Thieves stripped him, wounded him and left him half dead. The treatment of this man by a priest, Levite and a Samaritan is the focus for this reading. Jesus is answering the young lawyer's question, *"And who is my neighbour?"* Closely note the position and actions of each character in the parable.

"And by chance there came down a certain priest that way: and when he saw him, he passed by on the other side."

When the priest saw the injured man, he passed by on the other side. This man's injury speaks to the state of all mankind before Christ redeemed us from the curse of the Law. The effect of the Fall left us all stripped of our raiment of Light and wounded or broke us into pieces leaving us half dead. While people walk around with natural life (bios) there is no Eternal Life (zoe) until we are born again. Apart from the New Birth, one is half dead. The priest, in this case, is after the Old Covenant which is imperfect and cannot help this man. This man required a spiritual touch from a ministry equipped to do such. The *"other side"* is always the position of the old order.

The same applies to the Levite. Levites were the tribe from which the priests came in the Old Covenant. The Levite came and looked on him but also passed by on the other side. The imperfect priesthood cannot go beyond this man on the same side! The imperfection in this parable is similar to Moses (Number 27:12). Moses viewed the Promised Land but could not enter, so the Law enters not into life in Christ Jesus. Both the priest and the Levite saw this man. They picture the religious system that was in operation then and now, and it is both comfortable and incapable thus leaving one in such a state as long as the form and fashion of it remain intact. It is helpless to give sight to the blind, make the lame walk and restore sons to widows, all of which speak spiritually of the lack of Eternal Life and Its Power through Christ Jesus our Lord.

Notice this particular Samaritan carefully. He is not there *by chance* as the priest was or *at the place* as the Levite was but instead, he *journeyed*. Yes, he was on a journey. Samaria means watch tower or to keep, guard or protect. If one surveys this meaning more carefully, the attributes of a shepherd emerge. The Samaritan is an apparent stranger from a far country on a journey.

Next, the verse declares the Samaritan *came where he was*. Jesus is becoming crystal clear at this point. He was at the beginning with God but came where mankind was in his stripped, wounded, and half dead state. Just as Jesus looked on the multitude in His day and was moved with compassion, so was the certain Samaritan in this parable who *had compassion on this certain man*. This course of action is the great Shepherd Instinct and Manner in full operation. *"But when he saw the multitudes, he was moved with compassion on them, because they fainted, and were scattered abroad, as sheep having no shepherd"* (Matthew 9:36).

The certain Samaritan not only came where the victim was but had compassion on him. "He then *"went to him and bound up his wounds…"* (Luke 10:34). How personal this restorative act of love and kindness gets at this point. He not only came to the place where the man was but to the man personally. Jesus again emerges so beautifully from this point. In Luke 4, Jesus declared Himself as the One fulfilling Isaiah (Chapter 61:1) when He said, *"The Spirit of the Lord GOD is upon me… he hath sent me to bind up the brokenhearted…"* This man's *wounds* means broken in pieces as does broken-hearted. Only the Original Creator can heal this wound.

This parable speaks so mightily of the Redemptive Work of Christ Jesus. Just as this man's wounds were healed, our wounds were healed once for all by Christ Jesus on the Cross. As recorded in the Scriptures, *"But he was wounded for our transgressions, he was bruised for our iniquities: the chastisement of our peace was upon him, and with his stripes, we are healed"* (Isaiah 53:5). He came to us personally where we were while we were yet sinners and has borne our griefs and carried our sorrows. He bound our wounds by taking us into Himself and bearing our sin on His Cross.

Not only did the certain Samaritan, who so profoundly mirrors the Lord Jesus, bind up the man's wounds, he also poured in *oil and wine*. Both oil and wine are spiritual types that point to the Holy Spirit. Again, spiritual healing is the only remedy for his *wounds*. The prophet Joel (Chapter 2) declares the Lord will be jealous of His land and will pity His people. The prophet spoke concerning Jesus Christ our Lord. *"Yea, the LORD will answer and say unto his people, Behold, I will send you corn, and wine, and oil, and ye shall be satisfied therewith, and I will no more make you a reproach among the heathen:"* (Joel 2:19). In perspective, the Words of this prophecy concern the Day of the Lord where a fully restored Body rests and rules with Him.

This act of the Samaritan is part of and depicts the whole concerning Redemption. The purpose was not just to bring one back to natural health alone but also to afford the man to be kept in a new quality of Life after the Spirit. Hence, the spiritual symbols of pouring in oil and wine. Yes, that which is spiritual poured directly into the wound! This symbolism is what Jesus has done for us. Glory to His Name!

After binding the man's wounds and pouring in oil and wine, the certain Samaritan *set him on his beast.* Think about what a beast would mean in that day. It would simply be a vehicle. No other vehicle will do for us spiritually except **His Own**. The root meaning of the word beast is possession. We belong to Jesus; purchased with a price.

1 Corinthians 6:20 reads, *"For ye are bought with a price: therefore glorify God in your body, and in your spirit, which are God's."*

To reiterate, this is not a natural work only but a powerful parable wherein the Redemptive Work of Christ comes alive to the spiritual eyes and ears of the sincere believer. Parables carry hidden truths, and the Spirit of Truth desires to make them understandable to those followers of Christ who come apart unto Him. From a spiritual perspective, this man was not only healed but endued with power to sustain him from that point of restoration forward.

The next step in the restorative aid of the particular Samaritan is that he recovered *at an inn.* The Greek word used for the *inn* is different than found in Luke 2 where there was no room for Mary and Joseph in the inn. This inn was a public house for receiving strangers versus a lodging place. Sounds similar but there is a difference. In fact, there is a significant difference from a spiritual point of view.

The heavenly truth is that Jesus is a public House for receiving believers. Our registry changes the moment we are born again. As believers, we confess as those of Hebrews 11:13 that *we are strangers and pilgrims on the earth.* The Apostle Peter referred to us in the same manner. We are strangers on the earth but not strangers of the household of God where we are fellow-citizens of the saints (Ephesians 2:19).

Did you notice the man transported the Samaritan to the place where strangers are received? Consider this point. Although we read where the children of Israel walked out of Egypt, spiritually, the Word declares in Exodus 19:4, *"...how I bare you on eagles' wings, and brought you unto myself."* They were actually being borne of God while He simultaneously destroyed the Egyptians. Further, from the moment the Samaritan came to the man, the man was at his mercy. What a powerful position! If only we would allow Christ to have such control in our lives.

The Samaritan did not merely drop the man off at the inn; he also *took care of him.* Revisiting the shepherd nature of the particular Samaritan, we can recall how Jesus differentiated between the hireling and the shepherd. In John 10:13, Jesus said the hireling cares not for the sheep. On the other hand, He said, the shepherd would lay his life down for the sheep.

This example in this parable is so very Christ-like. The particular Samaritan had cared for the man before he left. He demonstrated his love. Religious people speak convincingly, but they are often void of acts of kindness. Kindness is becoming so rare until the world is satisfied to see a mere *random act* of it. Please! Jesus taught by this same example. He cares for us as Peter exclaimed.

He demonstrated His care for us by laying down His Life for the sheep of His pasture. He still cares so much for us that Peter reminds us that *we can cast all our care upon Him* (I Peter 5:7).

"And on the morrow when he departed, he took out two pence, and gave them to the host, and said unto him, take care of him; and whatsoever thou spendest more, when I come again, I will repay thee" (Luke 10:35). Up to and including this verse which begins on the morrow, we can account for two days. That stated, one can infer that a picture of work in righteousness is in full operation at this point. In Luke 13:32, Jesus responded to Herod with these Words, *"Go ye, and tell that fox, Behold, I cast out devils, and I do cures to day and to morrow, and the third day I shall be perfected."* Cures in progress!

Here it is easy to see that this Samaritan is yet another picture of our

Lord who was despised and rejected; nevertheless, He was the Savior of the world. John 14:3 reads, *"And if I go and prepare a place for you, I will come again, and receive you unto myself; that where I am, there ye may be also."* This indubitable Samaritan announced that he would *come again*. What would be happening in the meantime? This duration in the parable is for us to see that Christ Jesus was going to the Cross and preparing a place in Himself for His Church through His obedience unto death and perfection in the Resurrection on the third day.

Before his departure, the determined Samaritan *"took out two pence and gave them to the host, and said unto him, Take care of him; and whatsoever thou spendest more, when I come again, I will repay thee."* The Greek tells us *two pence* was a silver coin or denarius. The meaning of the word denarius is equal to ten. Ten is the Biblical Number for Law. The lawyer that Jesus was addressing in this parable (Luke 10: 25-19) illustrates the introduction to the higher law of the spirit of life in Christ Jesus. He was about to see with laser precision that the letter kills but the Spirit giveth life (2 Corinthians 3:6).

By the good Samaritan taking out *two pence*, he was demonstrating that the Law is now fulfilled and the sin debt fully paid. The whole purpose of the Law was that man would become aware of sin (Romans 7:7). The complete healing of the man in this parable became imminent because sin had no place for operation in him once the host received the two pence.

The two pence also were equal to the shekel of the sanctuary of Exodus 30: 12. *"When thou takest the sum of the children of Israel after their number, then shall they give every man a ransom for his soul unto the LORD, when thou numberest them; that there be no plague among them, when thou numberest them."* Yes, the same as the ransom money! It did not matter whether one was rich or poor, the amount of the ransom money was the same. Thank You, Jesus!

After Jesus, the Living Word, spoke this parable to this lawyer, he then asked him, *"Which now of these three, thinkest thou, was neighbor unto him that fell among the thieves?"* The choices were a priest, a Levite, or a certain Samaritan. Without acknowledging the certain Samaritan, the lawyer said, *"He that shewed mercy on him."* Jesus did not say, *"thou answered right"* as verse

28 states. Mercy speaks for Himself! In His Righteousness and without partiality in any form, He just said, *"Go, and do thou likewise."* Remember, Jesus did not do away with the Law but rather fulfilled It. That means it is finished or accomplished.

Prayerfully, we will not miss the awesome Power in this parable. Those skilled in the Law may be able to rehearse Law and answer correctly in matters of the Law, *but grace and truth came by Jesus Christ* (John 1:17). The lack of power in most ministry is the expectation that the Law can deliver the truth, but It cannot. People are constantly bombarded with Law whether intentional or not. Always remember that what speaks to the Law, the priest, and a Levite, cannot pass on the same side. Many leaders do not want to hurt the people of God, but they do not know the Truth and cannot help themselves or others. We cannot expect the religious system to do that which is impossible. On the same note, it is time to learn Christ!

By this parable and His Work in Righteousness, Jesus demonstrated that we could be doers and not hearers only. The beauty of mercy is that it is not only kindness shown toward another, but it partners with a genuine desire to help. Many times, people weary themselves by trying to be kind to others for carnal reasons. When Christ becomes resident within, the desire becomes equal to the act, and He then comes forth as Mercy. Pure Mercy! Be blessed, Neighbor!

Chapter Ten

Grace Knows the Enemy's Location and what it Means

"Now the Philistines gathered together their armies to battle, and were gathered together at Shochoh, which [belongeth] to Judah, and pitched between Shochoh and Azekah, in Ephesdammim." 1 Samuel 17:1

Enshrouded in the above verse is our spiritual enemy's exact location in our mind. The Philistines, Israel's staunch enemy, unknowingly left an important clue for detecting the position of the believer's spiritual enemy. In the face-off described in First Samuel Chapter 17, a young man yet a future king, faced a giant. Life or death. In powerful spiritual symbolism, the scene pictures the believer who is preparing to begin his journey of life in the Spirit. Before he can start, a giant enemy, Goliath, which symbolizes the carnal mind, must be destroyed with a work in righteousness where grace abounds.

The Philistines camped between *Shochoh* and *Azekah* in *Ephesdammim*. Shochoh means *bushy*. Its root meaning is *hedge* or *fence* as used in the Book of Job when the devil had to confess that Job had a hedge of protection placed by God that he could not penetrate without permission. Shochoh further means *Sukkot* which is the Feast of Booths or Feast of Tabernacles. This feast represents a believer entering full spiritual maturity.

Azekah means *dug-over*. The natural picture is one of tilling the earth. However, the spiritual symbol is in Hosea 10:12 which reads, *"Sow to yourselves in righteousness, reap in mercy; break up your fallow ground: for [it is] time to seek the LORD, till he come and rain righteousness upon you."* A prepared heart in earnest before God is the spiritual image that emerges.

Ephesdammin means *edge of blood*. The enemy encamps at a place where the believer's life in power and great grace are at stake. Leviticus 17:11 reads, *"The life of the flesh is in the blood..."* The spiritual mind knows that true life in Christ is at risk if the believer allows the enemy to overcome in his mind. Notice that the location of Ephesdammin is between the new convert (Azekah) and his place of maturity (Shochoh). Prayerfully, the urgency of seeing this truth is apparent.

Praise God for David who pictures Jesus Christ our Lord. Employing the tools of the spirit, a staff for comfort, five smooth stones *(grace)*, and a sling which is the same as the hangings made of fine linen or righteousness in the Tabernacle, a young man moved in the strength of God! With a spiritual eye, the believer can see that David moved in the power of the kingdom of God which is righteousness (the sling), peace (the staff) and joy (five stones or grace) in the Holy Ghost. As illustrated in the Book of 1 Samuel chapter 17 all we need are The Comforter, grace and an understanding that Jesus became righteousness for our sake. With one strike to the forehead, the giant (carnal mind) was demolished, and his enemies were scattered. One revelation of Jesus Christ and His Redemptive Work will destroy our carnal thinking and allow us to live a life of power and victory in the Spirit with great favor abounding!

I Samuel 17:1 *Now the Philistines gathered together their armies to battle, and were gathered together at Shochoh, which [belongeth] to Judah, and pitched between Shochoh and Azekah, in Ephesdammim.*
(The spiritual position of the Philistines as an enemy to Israel (believers) was between the new convert and his place of maturity in Christ).

EPHESDAMMIM = Edge of Blood

AZEKAH=Dug Over
Broken Up Earth (Fallow Ground)
PRINCIPLE: The Believer's Sincere Heart

SHOCHOH = Bushy
SUKKOT (Feast of Booths (Tabernacles)
PRINCIPLE: Spiritual Maturity in Christ

ENEMY
(Philistines)

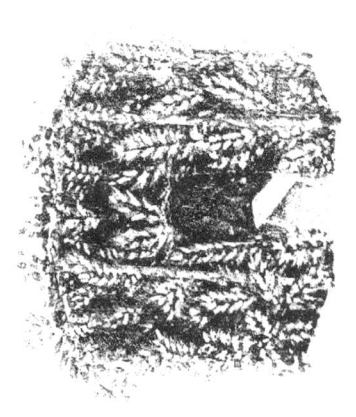

Hosea 10:12 Sow to yourselves in righteousness, reap in mercy; break up your fallow ground: for *it is* time to seek the LORD, till he come and rain righteousness upon you.

Zechariah 14:16 And it shall come to pass, *that* every one that is left of all the nations which came against Jerusalem shall even go up from year to year to worship the King, the LORD of hosts, and to keep the feast of tabernacles.

Chapter Eleven

A Carnal Ministry Hinders Grace

Grace is God's way of accomplishing His will in and through us rather than what many are trying to do by lording over His people in self-effort. There is a character in the Old Testament that is rarely noted but is a good example for exposing that which would staggeringly hinder God's grace. His name is Gaal from Judges Chapter 9, and he symbolizes carnal and powerless ministry. The writer's preference is to focus on the solution rather than the problem, but there are times when God's children need a heavenly spotlight shed on them when they are in gross darkness.

Gaal means to *detest* or *dislike intensely*. His name also has another meaning which is to reject. He is a classic picture of a ministry managed by its own Adamic strength and power. That is the fallen man with all his soul power. Gaal represents self-effort and self-righteousness at their peak. He is the perfect portrait of the current religious system. While this type of ministry detests our adversary, it refuses to yield entirely to the Power of the Cross and chooses instead to deal with the enemy in the strength, or lack thereof, of the fallen nature. For example, a ministry may be called "Healing Center" but is not Christ-centered and Spirit-filled. How would that ever afford the opportunity of spiritual maturity in Christ for God's people?

A Gaal ministry usually draws a huge crowd. Because such ministry is not powered by the Gospel which includes the power of God unto salvation and which burns the flesh and purges self-effort, there is absolutely no threat to the carnal, sensual, devilish nature the Gaal ministry lures. Simply detesting or hating sin is not enough here. What is important is to love God with the whole heart. A Gaal ministry hates the adversary so much until all its effort focuses on fighting him. The adversary rather than Christ is the central theme of such ministry. It is always about what flesh can do independent of God to put the adversary under the feet of the people. It will never, ever, ever, ever happen.

This type of ministry only hears mixture or a watered-down version of the Gospel. In either case, flesh is allowed to go head-on and unchecked toward an end of destruction. The pure Gospel is rarely ministered and if by chance It is, consider It disregarded because the stage is instantly reset for more flesh to go on parade. Gaal's signature ministry is in self-help and material gain. Ten points here; eight points there; twelve points when all else fails. People with a heart to follow Gaal will never be comfortable sitting under the preaching of the pure message of the Person and Work of the Lord Jesus Christ.

Following is an excerpt from Judges Chapter 9 which will provide insight into what is happening at the time of Gaal. The reader is encouraged to read Judges 9 in its entirety.

Reading: Judges 9:22-26

[22] "When Abimelech had reigned three years over Israel, [23] Then God sent an evil spirit between Abimelech and the men of Shechem; and the men of Shechem dealt treacherously with Abimelech: [24] That the cruelty [done] to the threescore and ten sons of Jerubbaal might come, and their blood be laid upon Abimelech their brother, which slew them; and upon the men of Shechem, which aided him in the killing of his brethren. [25] And the men of Shechem set liers in wait for him in the top of the mountains, and they robbed all that came along that way by them: and it was told Abimelech. 26 And Gaal the son of Ebed came with his brethren, and went over to Shechem: and the men of Shechem put their confidence in him."

Gaal was the son of Ebed whose name means *a slave.* Since he represents a powerless church in the false religious system, it is wise to glean from 2 Peter 2:17-19, which warns of false teachers. The Amplified Bible reads,

> These are springs without water and mists driven along before a tempest, for whom is reserved forever the gloom of darkness. For uttering loud boasts of folly, they beguile and lure with lustful desires of the flesh those who are barely escaping from them who are wrongdoers. They promise them liberty, when they themselves are the slaves of depravity and defilement-for by whatever anyone is made inferior or worse or is overcome, to that [person or thing] he is enslaved.

A Gaal ministry is helpless to free anyone. The freedom from spiritual slavery requires the supernatural power of Christ. He has accomplished it so why not walk in the perfect law of liberty.

Confidence in man is what set up Abimelech in the first place. First, it was Abimelech; now it is Gaal. More of the same problem is never the remedy! Some of the same people who once trusted in Abimelech are now ready to break away and do their own thing. Sound familiar? Same old wicked, powerless program with a new title which makes it appear to be on the Lord's side. Gaal detests Abimelech but wants to perpetuate his bondage. It is still about man and not God! The whole desperate situation then and now can be easily avoided if men would trust in God. Verse 26 above says the men of Shechem now put their confidence in Gaal.

One of the meanings of *promotion* is to toss to and fro? Man does not have a promotion for you, precious people of God. Psalm 118:8-9 reminds us, *"It is better to trust in the LORD than to put confidence in man. It is better to trust in the LORD than to put confidence in princes."* Gaal is not the answer! Christ is the answer! Gaal has the same ulterior motive as Abimelech. He wants the people to be *under his hand*. The hand of man is no protection from the evil one. It is entirely deficient yet claims to provide a means of refuge that it never possessed. Please hear the Voice of God!

> *"And they went out into the fields, and gathered their vineyards, and trode [the grapes], and made merry, and went into the house of their god, and did eat and drink, and cursed Abimelech." Judges 9:27*

Once they reached their level of confidence in Gaal, there was a celebration. Now that the people are snuggled deeply in disobedience, everything is perverted. The problem with this party is that it is a substitute for a God-ordained celebration known as the Feast of Tabernacles. How do we know this? The harvest from the vineyard gives it away. Deuteronomy 16:13-15 reads,

> Thou shalt observe the feast of tabernacles seven days, after that thou hast gathered in thy corn and thy wine: And thou that rejoice in thy feast, thou, and thy son, and thy daughter, and thy manservant, and thy maidservant, and the Levite, the stranger, and the fatherless, and the widow, that are within thy gates. Seven days shalt thou keep a solemn feast unto the LORD thy God in the place which the LORD shall choose: because the LORD thy God shall bless thee in all thine increase, and in all the works of thine hands, therefore thou shalt surely rejoice.

If the people practice the exclusion of God, there is no celebration.

More on the Feast of Tabernacles is found in Leviticus 23:33-44. However, from the earlier reference from the Book of Deuteronomy, it is evident that people are far out of the Will of God. Instead of keeping the God-ordained feast, they are in the temple *of their god* eating and drinking and cursing. From what we just read from Deuteronomy, this should be a time of blessing. Minds and hearts should be to God. From Leviticus, one can see they should be dwelling in booths instead of in the house of a false god. As with any generation that turns from the True and Living God, the blessing of God will not be upon it.

> *Judges 9:28 "And Gaal the son of Ebed said, Who [is] Abimelech, and who [is] Shechem, that we should serve him? [is] not [he] the son of Jerubbaal? And Zebul his officer? Serve the men of Hamor the father of Shechem: for why should we serve him?"*

> *Judges 9:29 "And would to God this people were under my hand! Then would I remove Abimelech. And he said to Abimelech, Increase thine army, and come out."*

As long as the Adamic, carnal nature is ruling, there will always be rebellion and a power struggle. Assess the condition in almost any church where the Gospel is not present or preached. Also, keep in mind if the Redemptive Work of the Lord Jesus Christ is not before the people constantly, it will be easy to see multitudes of Abimelechs and Gaals. Count the number of churches in your local area, and you will get a good idea of the magnitude of the force of the carnal nature. There are too many churches breaking off and starting anew with the same old lifeless power behind them. This false system is on a timetable, and it is just a matter of time before God avenges His Perfect Plan and sets things in order.

Notice verse 29 above, many leaders today believe that having enough heads to count or people in the pews is the answer to this problem. The emphasis of this book is that we all need the authority of Christ in order to deal with the forces we face today. Again, we need power, not "head counts" for this situation! Further, threats to the adversary *to increase his army and come out are useless. "The weapons of our warfare are not carnal"* as stated in 2 Corinthians 10:4. The lack of power and authority is how the adversary can secure such a stronghold in so many lives and ministries.

Threats and talk are ineffective and are mere powerless shots at the enemy as many will come to find out. Carnality against carnality accomplishes nothing. The end result is dust flying, and the serpent is able to get a good meal in such situations. Remember, he was cursed to eat dust (Genesis 3:14). When one fails to walk in the Spirit, he becomes *"devil's food."* Carnality is synonymous with dust. Flesh, too, is synonymous with dust. There is a life that is higher!

"And would to God this people were under my hand! then would I remove Abimelech." Gaal made promises he was unable to keep. Clearly, the Bible relates whose voice is behind such a promise.

For instance, there is a similar sound to the promise the devil used to try to tempt Jesus. *"All this power will I give thee, and the glory of them: for that is delivered unto me; and to whomsoever I will give it, If thou therefore wilt worship me, all shall be thine."* (Luke 4:6-7). A Gaal ministry does not have the power to remove Abimelech as he boasted. Just like the devil has nothing, neither does a powerless Gaal ministry. No matter how many people are under his hand, Gaal or no other leader has the ability to handle this force in his own strength. It is time for men and women everywhere to get an understanding of the victory of the Cross and live in it by faith. If not, at best one can only aspire to become a pawn for empty, meaningless ministry.

Reading Judges 9:30-38

[30] "And when Zebul the ruler of the city heard the words of Gaal the son of Ebed, his anger was kindled. [31] And he sent messengers unto Abimelech privily, saying, Behold, Gaal the son of Ebed and his brethren be come to Shechem; and, behold, they fortify the city against thee. [32] Now therefore up by night, thou and the people that [is] with thee, and lie in wait in the field: [33] And it shall be, [that] in the morning, as soon as the sun is up, thou shalt rise early, and set upon the city: and, behold, [when] he and the people that [is] with him come out against thee, then mayest thou do to them as thou shalt find occasion. [34] And Abimelech rose up, and all the people that [were] with him, by night, and they laid wait against Shechem in four companies. [35] And Gaal the son of Ebed went out, and stood in the entering of the gate of the city: and Abimelech rose up, and the people that [were] with him, from lying in wait. [36] And when Gaal saw the people, he said to Zebul, Behold, there come people down from the top of the mountains. And Zebul said unto him, Thou seest the shadow of the mountains as [if they were] men. [37] And Gaal spake again and said, See there come people down by the middle of the land, and another company come along by the plain of Meonenim. [38] Then said Zebul unto him, <u>Where [is] now thy mouth</u>, wherewith thou saidst, Who [is] Abimelech, that we should serve him? [is] not this the people that thou hast despised? go out, I pray now, and fight with them."

As stated earlier, we now see how shallow talk really is. <u>"Where [is] now thy mouth?"</u> Here are the loud bursts of folly aforementioned. There is only one mouth capable of overthrowing Abimelech and what he represents, and the prophet Isaiah leaves no doubt that the Capable One is the Messiah.

"There shall come a rod out of the stem of Jesse, and a Branch shall grow out of His roots: And the spirit of the LORD shall rest upon him, the spirit of wisdom and understanding, the spirit of counsel and might, the spirit of knowledge and of the fear of the LORD; And shall make him of quick understanding in the fear of the LORD: and he shall not judge after the sight of his eyes neither reprove after the hearing of his ears: But with righteousness shall he judge the poor, and reprove with equity for the meek of the earth: and he shall smite the earth with the rod of his mouth, and with the breath of his lips shall he slay the wicked" (Isaiah 11: 1-4).

Judges 9:39 "And Gaal went out before the men of Shechem, and fought with Abimelech."

Judges 9:40 "And Abimelech chased him, and he fled before him, and many were overthrown [and] wounded, [even] unto the entering of the gate."

The Book of Judges chapter 9 provides a Biblical picture of the guaranteed outcome of anyone who chooses to fight in his own strength. Expect to be chased by the enemy! As many have noted concerning the armor of God, there is no armor for the back. If there is a chase, one is at full, defenseless exposure to the enemy. This force is not out-run but is out-done through Christ! It boils down to the simple question of whether we would rather overcome or be overthrown. It is evident a curse for disobedience is in operation because the blessing of God is that He will strike down our enemies that rise up against us before our faces. Remember, *"They shall come out at us one way but will flee before us seven ways"* (Deuteronomy 28:7). In light of Judges 9: 39-40 and Deuteronomy 28:7 and, as the common catch phrase goes, "Something is wrong with this picture?"

Judges 9:41 "And Abimelech dwelt at Arumah: and Zebul thrust out Gaal and his brethren, that they should not dwell in Shechem."

Abimelech dwelt at Arumah which means *self-exaltation*. Well, this brings us back to the earlier points in this chapter. Self-exaltation is the catalyst for this whole false system. Grace is shut out! Reading 2 Thessalonians 2:1-4 at this time is a good idea. May the eyes of the reader's understanding be flooded with the Light of Christ.

> "Now we beseech you, brethren, by the coming of our Lord Jesus Christ, and by our gathering together unto him, That ye be not soon shaken in mind, or be troubled, neither by spirit, nor by word nor by letter as from us, as that the day of Christ is at hand. Let no man deceive you by any means: for that day shall not come, except there come a falling away first, and that man of sin be revealed, the son of perdition: Who opposeth and exalteth himself above all that is called God, or that is worshipped; so that he as God sitteth in the temple of God, shewing himself that he is God."

First Corinthians informs us that we are the temple of God (1 Corinthians 3:16). The day of Christ is His appearing. Appearing is synonymous with unveiling or uncovering or His being revealed <u>in</u> us rather than <u>to</u> us. It is time to make this whole issue very personal and examine ourselves to see who sits on the throne in our heart. Is it Christ Who has the right or the Gaal mentality in us as though he is God (2 Thessalonians 2:3-4)? Oh, the falling away will definitely come first. The only way the man of sin (Adam, the fallen man), will be revealed is for the flesh or carnal nature to *"fall away."* The brightness of the coming of the Lord or a revelation of Who He is in us is what breaks the outer man and reveals the true, hidden man of the heart.

For another picture of the power of God's dealings with His people through His Son, think about how Gideon defeated the Midianites. Their weapons were not "carnal" but mighty through God to the pulling down of strongholds! Think about it! Their weapons included a trumpet, empty pitchers, and lamps within the pitchers. All they had to do was obey the instructions of God through Gideon, their leader. Once outside the enemy's camp, they sounded their trumpets.

The trumpet simply speaks to a clear-sounding Word from the Lord. A clear-sounding Word will always center on Christ. They then broke their pitchers and held their lamps in their hands. They stood in their respective places around the enemy's camp and proclaimed, *"The sword of the LORD and of Gideon."* The enemy's host ran (Judges 7:16-21)! The point driven home is that the lamps were inside the pitchers. The broken pitcher is like the falling away of the flesh or the carnal man. There is a Lamp inside us, and His Name is Jesus! He will be seen by every eye when the flesh falls from around us. Hallelujah!

Judges 9:42-47 states:

> [42] "And it came to pass on the morrow, that the people went out into the field; and they told Abimelech. [43] And he took the people, and divided them into three companies, and laid wait in the field, and looked, and, behold, the people [were] come forth out of the city; and he rose up against them, and smote them. [44] And Abimelech, and the company that [was] with him, rushed forward, and stood in the entering of the gate of the city: and the two [other] companies ran upon all [the people] that [were] in the fields, and slew them. [45] And Abimelech fought against the city all that day; and he took the city, and slew the people that [was] therein, and beat down the city, and sowed it with salt. [46] "And when all the men of the tower of Shechem heard [that], they entered into an hold of the house of the god Berith. [47] And it was told Abimelech, that all the men of the tower of Shechem were gathered together."

Before we continue with the last verses, it would be beneficial to note the stops of Abimelech with great care. Notice the force of evil in full swing. We have seen that he went to a place called Arumah, which means *self-exaltation*. Now he is about to make another move. He and his henchmen are about to go to a mount or high place, and the name is significant from a spiritual standpoint. Additionally, take careful consideration of what he does at this stop and weigh it against the Word of God. Cautiously, let us read the following verses now.

> And Abimelech gat him up to mount Zalmon, he and all the people that [were] with him; and Abimelech took an axe in his hand, and cut down a bough from the trees, and took it, and laid [it] on his shoulder, and said unto the people that [were] with him, What

ye have seen me do, make haste, [and] do as I [have done].

Judges 9:48

And all the people likewise cut down every man his bough, and followed Abimelech, and put [them] to the hold, and set the hold on fire upon them; so that all the men of the tower of Shechem died also, about a thousand men and women.

Judges 9:49

Mount Zalmon means *phantom or illusion*. To appreciate and embrace what the Holy Spirit is saying here let us go back and look at a verse above from Judges 9:36 which states, *"And when Gaal saw the people, he said to Zebul, Behold, there come people down from the top of the mountains. And Zebul said unto him, Thou seest the shadow of the mountains as [if they were] men."* Gaal was actually seeing men, but Zebul tried to make him believe it was something else. Zebul was an agent for the enemy and knew the ambush was in place because he was the one who had warned Abimelech of Gaal's rebellion. The shadow as used here means *defense or covering*. The enemy agents are skilled at making things appear to be for our good when they are intended to do us deadly harm. Hear it well.

The biggest problem with this place that Abimelech has come to is that Zalmon is the same as used in Genesis 1:26 when God said, *"Let us make man in our image; after our likeness..."* The word *"image"* and Zalmon mean one and the same. From the start, Abimelech wanted to be ruler over the people. Not just any ruler but a ruler in the place of the Most High God. His motive will never change, and he can only have power in people who will allow him to rule over them. Spiritually consider who we are answering to in the Name of Jesus!

Gaal nor any other rebellious minister can handle this force. If he had only understood the power of trusting in God alone, the entire sequence of events would have changed. The Book of Judges would not be the same. Grace facilitates great exploits in supernatural power shattering all the work of the enemy. Today, God's people need to understand the importance of keeping the Feast of Tabernacles. Since these people were not honoring the feast as prescribed or commanded by God in Judges 9, note the very boughs of trees they should have been using for God's purpose were being used to burn them in their faulty shelter in the house of their idol god. In a nutshell, if we do not receive Jesus Christ, His Person and His Work as all and in all, the very protective Power that He is will be used against us by an adversary to destroy us. Think about it! How often is the Word of God being quoted out of context and used as a scare tactic instead of life and health and peace to His people while they are under the "protection" of their idols? Too many ministries are becoming idols. Again, Gaal is not in charge. Jesus Christ is Lord of all. We have one Lord, and He is God. Keep the Feast or be destroyed.

Grace's Gentle Warning

Galatians 5:4 "Christ is become of no effect unto you, whosoever of you are justified by **the law; ye are fallen from grace."**

Romans 11:6 "And if by grace, then **is it** *no more of works: otherwise grace is no more grace. But if* **it be** *of works, then is it no more grace: otherwise work is no more work."*

CHAPTER TWELVE

GRACE FACILITATES GOD'S PURPOSE

"That is, They which are the children of the flesh, these are not the children of God: but the children of the promise are counted for the seed." Romans 9:8

"(For the children being not yet born, neither having done any good or evil, that the purpose of God according to election might stand, not of works, but of him that calleth;) [12] *It was said unto her, The elder shall serve the younger.* [13] *As it is written, Jacob have I loved, but Esau have I hated." Romans 9:11-13*

That the purpose of God according to election might stand, not of works, but of him that calleth is a Supreme Fact that every believer must come to terms with in their heart. The gift of grace facilitates God's Purpose. God's ways are not our ways, and His thoughts are not our thoughts. Christ must be our very Life so that the wisdom of God works within. If not, the precious Gift that He is will be nullified because of a lack of wisdom and unbelief. For instance, to the natural mind, verse 11 above, may easily seem that Esau was being picked on. The spiritual mind would instead focus on the eternal purpose of God. The two brothers, Esau and Jacob, provide spiritual clarity in that the flesh is the enemy of God and cannot please Him.

Esau speaks to the flesh with its carnal mentality, and Jacob speaks to promise or that which is spiritual. The Prophet Malachi states, "Esau was hated by God" (Malachi 1:3). *"Hated"* is also translated *"enemy"* in several Scriptures. The contrast is evident in Galatians 5:17 which declares, *"For the flesh lusteth against the Spirit, and the Spirit against the flesh: and these are contrary the one to the other: so that ye cannot do the things that ye would."*

Genesis 25 describes Esau as a cunning hunter, a man of the field. Jesus taught that the field is the world. James 4:4 states that friendship of the world is also enmity against God. Esau's name means *hairy*. At birth, he came out red and as a hairy garment. The unmistakable earthy man! The root meaning of "hairy" is to *bristle with horror*. Therefore, to many, his description is equivalent to a garment of fear. On the other hand, the believer's garment (mantle or covering) is Light. Light is synonymous with Love, the Gift. The same Wonderful Being is our Lord and Savior Jesus Christ, our Eternal Covering with His bounty of grace.

Esau bears no resemblance to the Beloved Only Begotten Son of God. Instead, he represents the Adamic nature, the carnal man who is bound to the world system. His whole meaning in life is to cunningly hunt for and eat flesh. His soul demanded immediate fulfillment and lusted for red pottage or carnal Adamic sustenance. His birthright, which speaks to the believer's spiritual inheritance in Christ, became insignificant to him because his soul was in control. Grace was at the door of his heart (spirit), and he preferred to satisfy the soul: his own mind, will and emotions. "...*The elder shall serve the younger*" (Genesis 25:23). 1 Corinthians 15:48 reads, "*As [is] the earthy, such [are] they also that are earthy...*" Also, John 3:6 corresponds, "*That which is born of the flesh is flesh...*"

> And Jacob sod pottage: and Esau came from the field, and he was faint: And Esau said to Jacob, Feed me, I pray thee, with that same red pottage; for I am faint: therefore was his name called Edom. And Jacob said, Sell me this day thy birthright. And Esau said, Behold, I am at the point to die: and what profit shall this birthright do to me? And Jacob said, Swear to me this day; and he sware unto him: and he sold his birthright unto Jacob. Then Jacob gave Esau bread and pottage of lentiles; and he did eat and drink, and rose up, and went his way: thus Esau despised his birthright.
>
> Genesis 25: 29-34

According to The Companion Bible, there are three major parts of the birthright. They include the following:

(a) The Father's Supremacy and Blessing

Went to Jacob (Genesis 27) and Judah (Genesis 49:8);

(b) A Double Portion Went to Joseph (Genesis 48) and

(1Chronicles 5:1-2)

(c) The Domestic Priesthood

Which after going to the firstborn of each family was vested in Levi for the whole nation (Numbers 3:6, 12).

As noted previously, the carnal man (Esau) is satisfied only by the flesh. The Companion Bible also states that the word "birthright" translates "ware" or "merchandize." All the merchandizing in the church today is a symptom of a much larger problem! Adam, Esau, or Edom all speak to the earthy man. The birthright and the blessing are contingent upon each other.

Birthright means first born. Spiritually, that means conforming to the image of the Son of God, the Firstborn of many brethren. (Romans 8:29). The carnal man knows at heart that he is unable to live up to the responsibilities inherent in the birthright. Some of these responsibilities include walking or living in the Spirit, believing on Him Whom God hath sent, receiving His grace, and living by faith. Hence his lustful soul must die if he is to be an obedient son. Just like the carnal ones that would come after him, the idol of Esau's heart demanded a celebration, *and he did eat and drink, and rose up, and went his way, thus despising his birthright.*

"Neither be ye idolaters, as [were] some of them; as it is written, The people sat down to eat and drink, and rose up to play." 1 Corinthians 10:7

"That is, They which are the children of the flesh, these are not the children of God: but the children of the promise are counted for the seed.

(For the children being not yet born, neither having done any good or evil, that the purpose of God according to election might stand, not of works, but of him that calleth;) It was said unto her, The elder shall serve the younger. As it is written, Jacob have I loved, but Esau have I hated" Romans 9:8, 11-13

"...and Jacob [was] a plain man, dwelling in tents" Genesis 25:27

Again, we visit the Supreme fact *"that the purpose of God according to election might stand, not of works, but of him that calleth."* Jacob's brother, Esau, was divinely used in Scripture to show us the self-destruction and futile effort of the carnal man in relation to pleasing God. Jacob, on the other hand, is divinely used to show how the flesh can overcome by the power of the Spirit. Observe grace in action.

Jacob, *a plain man*. The word plain is the same as "perfect" used of Job. Job Chapter One describes Job as a man perfect and upright, and one that feared God, and eschewed evil. He speaks to the renewed spirit. God is spirit (John 4:24). The seed was called in Isaac (Romans 9:7), and the seed is Christ (Galatians 3:16). Jacob is the one that God loved (Malachi 1:2). *"But ye are not in the flesh, but in the Spirit, if so be that the Spirit of God dwell in you. Now if any man have not the Spirit of Christ, he is none of his"* (Romans 8:9). Jacob, later called Israel or *God prevails*, (Genesis 32:28), speaks to the heavenly.

1 Corinthians 15:48 "... and as [is] the heavenly, such [are] they also that are heavenly."

1 Corinthians 15:49 "...we shall also bear the image of the heavenly."

John 3:6 "... and that which is born of the Spirit is spirit."

Christ Jesus has been made unto us all that we need to overcome. What grace we have in that all we need to do is abide in Him Who has already overcome the evil one. Christ is *wisdom, righteousness, sanctification, and redemption* to all who believe (1 Corinthians 1:30). Each believer is a *plain* man who is perfect and upright in Him. Fear God and refuse evil! His Holy Spirit will lead, teach, and equip just for the asking!

Grace's Spotlight on Law

Galatians 6:13 "For neither they themselves who are circumcised keep the law; but desire to have you circumcised, that they may glory in your flesh."

1 Timothy 1:9 "Knowing this, that the law is not made for a righteous man, but for the lawless and disobedient, for the ungodly and for sinners, for unholy and profane, for murderers of fathers and murderers of mothers, for manslayers."

Titus 3:9 "But avoid foolish questions, and genealogies, and contentions, and strivings about the law; for they are unprofitable and vain."

Hebrews 7:19 "For the law made nothing perfect, but the bringing in of a better hope did; by the which we draw nigh unto God."

CHAPTER THIRTEEN

DECEPTION: AN ARCHENEMY OF GRACE

"And the LORD God planted a garden eastward in Eden; and there he put the man whom he had formed." Genesis 2:8

Our loving Creator planted a garden eastward in Eden where He placed the man He had formed. The root meaning of *garden* is to *defend, cover, surround or hedge about something*. The first man's habitation was a place of protection, plenty, and peace, as well as, a full expression of God's Substance within him and surrounding him. The garden was situated eastward in *Eden* which means *pleasure*. Eden comes from a meaning so intensely rich that it takes such words as luxury, dainty, delight, finery to help one grasp its essence. What a glorious state of existence and environment of an unimpeded relationship between God and man!

The garden encapsulates unfathomable truths. Song of Solomon sheds light on God's intent for it and the man He put there. Song of Solomon 4:12, 16 reads, *"A garden enclosed is my sister, my spouse; a spring shut up, a fountain sealed. Awake, O north wind; and come, thou south; blow upon my garden, that the spices thereof may flow out. Let my beloved come into his garden, and eat his pleasant fruits."* An omniscient God knew the Fall would occur and the garden, though a place, ultimately spoke to Christ and His Church.

Genesis 2:9 "And out of the ground made the LORD God to grow every tree that is pleasant to the sight, and good for food; the tree of life also in the midst of the garden, and the tree of knowledge of good and evil."

Notice that the trees were pleasant to the sight and good for food. The Word of God contains an incalculable amount of revelation for the hearing ear. It is critical to note the order of emphasis God placed on the purpose of the trees. First, they were *"pleasant to the sight."* Above, it indicates that Eden already means pleasure; however, God saw fit to magnify the pleasure that the trees could afford "the sight."

Let us shift from the trees for a moment and focus on what God means by *sight*. The Hebrew meaning and translation for *sight is appearance* or vision. Vision in this sense relates to the supernatural. The description is *to see, look at, inspect, perceive, consider*. The words perceive and consider both take on a more significant meaning than simply beholding a thing with the natural eye. They connote insight. To every overcomer, it should be apparent that we are now on higher ground in thought.

Next, Scriptures state that the trees were *"good for food."* Everything God made He had already declared "good" yet again we find Divine emphasis where the trees are concerned. The word good used here allies itself with terms such as *pleasant* and *agreeable* in capturing God's thought in His description of the trees. The food provided by the trees was not only pleasing to the appetite but apparently had a satisfying quality within it that was all sufficient making it most agreeable to the man.

Two particular trees were distinct from the others. In the midst of the garden were the tree of life and the tree of the knowledge of good and evil. For the moment let us focus on the latter. God gave concise instructions to the man regarding the tree of the knowledge of good and evil. "And the LORD God took the man, and put him into the garden of Eden to dress it and to keep it. *And the LORD God commanded the man, saying, "Of every tree of the garden thou mayest freely eat: But of the tree of the knowledge of good and evil, thou shalt not eat of it: for in the day that thou eatest thereof thou shalt surely die"* (Genesis 2:16-17). True then, true now.

God gave the man a woman. The woman, Eve, was beguiled by the serpent and ate of the forbidden tree of the knowledge of good and evil. She gave of the fruit thereof to Adam, her husband. Together, they speak to the spirit (inner man) and soul (mind, will, and emotions). Adam represents the spirit and Eve represents the soul. The Apostle Paul embraced this analogy when he warned the Church at Corinth of the spiritual significance of Eve's act of disobedience. He told them, *"But I fear, lest by any means, as the serpent beguiled Eve through his subtilty, so your minds should be corrupted from the simplicity that is in Christ"* (2 Corinthians 11:3). Notice the Apostle Paul linked "minds" directly to Eve. The deceiver targets and can only get a foothold in the mind. Let us revisit the deception.

> Now the serpent was more subtil than any beast of the field which the LORD God had made. And he said unto the woman, Yea, hath God said, Ye shall not eat of every tree of the garden? And the woman said unto the serpent, We may eat of the fruit of the trees of the garden: But of the fruit of the tree which is in the midst of the garden, God hath said, Ye shall not eat of it, neither shall ye touch it, lest ye die. And the serpent said unto the woman, Ye shall not surely die: For God doth know that in the day ye eat thereof, then your eyes shall be opened, and ye shall be as gods, knowing good and evil. And when the woman saw that the tree was good for food, and that it was pleasant to the eyes, and a tree to be desired to make one wise, she took of the fruit thereof, and did eat, and gave also unto her husband with her; and he did eat. And the eyes of them both were opened, and they knew that they were naked; and they sewed fig leaves together, and made themselves aprons.
>
> Genesis 3:1-7

Subtle is a perfect word to describe the serpent. When hedged in a garden surrounded by and filled with all that is pleasant and safe, one becomes victim to cunning persuasion which hates God and his perfect creation and slithers in through the only penetrable entry, the mind. Sadly, it happens too readily in the lives of many believers. Our position in Christ means we are back in our Heavenly Father's Presence and favor, and despite the pleasantness and spiritual power, deceit vies with truth in minds and hearts. Too often the deceit is engaged instead of casting it out.

God had a Divine Order or Precedence by the way man, who is spirit first, was to acknowledge and use the trees He planted. This writer refers to it as Eden's Edict. First, God said the trees were *"...pleasant to the sight and secondly, good for food..."* After the cunning serpent beguiled Eve, she "saw" something very different and changed God's Order in her heart because of her distorted, erroneous, lowly, carnal, view.

> "And when the woman saw that the tree was good for food, and that it was pleasant to the eyes, and a tree to be desired to make one wise, she took of the fruit thereof, and did eat, and gave also unto her husband with her; and he did eat."

The trees that were once foremost pleasant to the sight and spoke to their ability to perceive spiritually and accurately were now ineffective. All things had become carnal! The new order for them was first *"good for food."* In order words, things had to appeal to the flesh first, and spiritual things were no longer relevant. Praise God for Jesus being Spirit-led when the tempter came trying to capitalize on His hunger after fasting forty days. Knowing the difference between that which is spiritual and that which is carnal or that which is temporal and that which is eternal, He overcame. Spirit first!

Secondly, Eve "saw" the tree of the knowledge of good and evil was *"pleasant to the eyes."* Did you note how the deception changed the Word of God in her being? Again, God said *"pleasant to the sight,"* and it was <u>first</u> in His Order. Now, she heard, *pleasant to the eyes*. The words *"sight"* and *"eyes"* carry two different meanings in this context and two different words are used to teach us. *Eyes* speak to natural sight in this passage. Be most particular to note that all spiritual things have now departed.

Further, note that after her deception she "saw" something that God did not mention in Genesis 2:9. Now added was *"...a tree to be desired to make one wise."* The actual intent of God for a thing was now shrouded in carnality. All of a sudden, there is a "desire" that was unknown previously. In the spirit all sufficiency is of God; therefore, a desire for something other than God apparently arose from another source. Referring to the Apostle Paul's address to the Corinthians, his fear was they would hear another gospel and receive another Jesus not preached to them.

The deception placed an unnecessary burden on the man and woman.

Consequently, they had to attempt to figure things out instead of walking with God in the "cool" or spirit of the day and operating in full spiritual discernment. No longer spiritually cognizant of God's purpose for the trees, Adam and Eve used the leaves of a fig tree to cover their nakedness. They hid from God as if that was actually possible. God loves His creation so much that encrypted in Adam's response to God's call to him is a powerful truth. God is love. Adam responded, *"I heard thy voice in the garden, and I was afraid, because I was naked; and I hid myself"* (Genesis 3:10). The Hebrew word for "hid" is love as found in Deuteronomy 33: 3, "Yea, he loved the people…"

Every believer must know that God's love has not changed, and He has restored mankind through the obedience of the last Adam, Jesus Christ our Lord. Nothing can separate us from the love of Christ! Romans 8: 35, 37-39 assures:

> Who shall separate us from the love of Christ? shall tribulation, or distress, or persecution, or famine, or nakedness, or peril, or sword? Nay, in all these things we are more than conquerors through him that loved us. For I am persuaded, that neither death, nor life, nor angels, nor principalities, nor powers, nor things present, nor things to come, Nor height, nor depth, nor any other creature, shall be able to separate us from the love of God, which is in Christ Jesus our Lord.

Genesis 3:24 reads, *"So he drove out the man; and he placed at the east of the garden of Eden Cherubims, and a flaming sword which turned every way, to keep the way of the tree of life."* There is a common but false perception that because the man was driven out, the garden no longer exists. We just read that a flaming sword is keeping the way of the tree of life. Spiritually speaking, the Spirit of the fulfilled Word of God is maintaining the way of the Tree of Life.

Often the letter which kills is "ministered;" however, when the Spirit of the Word ministers in power, it is clear that Eden speaks to our position in Christ. Second Corinthians 3:6 tells us that God, *"…hath made us able ministers of the new testament; not of the letter, but of the spirit: for the letter killeth, but the spirit giveth life."* The Prophet Joel describes this same able *ministry* in Chapter 2:3 when he saw, *"A fire devoureth before them; and behind them a flame burneth: the land is as the garden of Eden before them, and behind them a desolate wilderness; yea, and nothing shall escape them."* Our God is a consuming fire. He goes before us and is our Rear Guard. Christ Jesus is the Way of the Spirit in which we travel, and as we pass through in Him in our ascent, nothing is behind that we ever wish to return to. Eden and all it speaks to remains in its pristine fullness in Christ.

The serpent's method of operating never changes. Be ever mindful of this fact. Whether the wicked one presents as the serpent, devil, adversary, accuser, or simply and most often, the carnal mind, he will always employ the same method of appealing to the lust of the flesh, the lust of the eyes and the pride of life. First John 2:16 reads, *"For all that is in the world, the lust of the flesh, and the lust of the eyes, and the pride of life, is not of the Father, but is of the world."*

As seen earlier, The Apostle Paul warned the Corinthians with love, and this carries the same message. Through Christ, refuse to allow the deception of the carnal mind to corrupt the simplicity that is found only in Him. Remember, *"But every man is tempted, when he is drawn away of his own lust, and enticed. Then when lust has conceived, it brings forth sin: and sin, when it is finished, brings forth death"* (James 1:14-15). May we all stop blaming a devil whose works were destroyed when the Son of God was manifested (I John 3:8) and rather put on the Lord Jesus Christ, and make no provision for the flesh, to *fulfill the lusts thereof* (Romans 13:14). Keep in mind, *"This I say then, Walk in the Spirit, and ye shall not fulfill the lust of the flesh"* (Galatians 5:16).

Chapter Fourteen

Grace Causes Accusers to Vanish

Scripture Reading: John 8: 1-11

¹But Jesus went to the Mount of Olives. ² Now early in the morning He came again into the temple, and all the people came to Him; and He sat down and taught them. ³ Then the scribes and Pharisees brought to Him a woman caught in adultery. And when they had set her in the midst, ⁴ they said to Him, "Teacher, this woman was caught in adultery, in the very act. ⁵ Now Moses, in the law, commanded us that such should be stoned. But what do You say?" ⁶ This they said, testing Him, that they might have something of which to accuse Him. But Jesus stooped down and wrote on the ground with His finger, as though He did not hear. ⁷ So when they continued asking Him, He raised Himself up and said to them, "He who is without sin among you, let him throw a stone at her first." ⁸ And again He stooped down and wrote on the ground. ⁹ Then those who heard it, being convicted by their conscience, went out one by one, beginning with the oldest even to the last. And Jesus was left alone, and the woman standing in the midst. ¹⁰ When Jesus had raised Himself up and saw no one but the woman, He said to her, "Woman, where are those accusers of yours? Has no one condemned you?" ¹¹ She said, "No one, Lord." And Jesus said to her, "Neither do I condemn you; go and sin no more."

Mercy! The scribes and Pharisees or the embodiment of Law confronted Jesus with a woman accused adultery. How Jesus dealt with this situation is another glaring example of grace and truth in full operation. "Law" demanded an answer and Jesus responded. Always be mindful that Jesus is now operating in the Spirit without measure. He is aware that the letter kills but the Spirit gives life. This situation did not pose a problem for Him at all. He simply implemented Himself into the situation. Grace and truth are passengers from His heavenly journey. He was sent to deliver them both intact.

An adulterous woman caught in the very act should be stoned according to the Law. There she was set in the midst, fully accessible to the full wave of wrath, the object of humiliation yet the subject of two different dispensations. Teacher, what have you got to say in the face of Mosaic Law?

Actually, the scribes and Pharisees were as much interested in accusing Jesus as the woman. Without a sound, Jesus stooped and wrote on the ground with His finger. Jesus never expended energy for naught. By Him stooping down, there is a glimpse of his mission according to Ephesians 4:9-10, *"He that descended is the same also that ascended far above all heavens, that he might fill all things. (Now that he ascended, what is it but that he also descended first into the lower parts of the earth)?"* One must understand that the Word became Flesh. Stooping conveys the act of going from a high place to a lower one.

The last time the finger of God wrote was in Exodus 31:18 which states, *"And he gave unto Moses, when he had made an end of communing with him upon mount Sinai, two tables of testimony, tables of stone, written with the finger of God."* Now Jesus, God with us, was writing again! Keep in mind that His constant companions are grace and truth. The scribes and Pharisees continued to ask Jesus for a response, and He made another gesture that continued to speak of His Mission. He lifted up Himself! His Mission always at the forefront of His actions.

Jesus once declared, *"Destroy this temple, and in three days <u>I will raise it up</u>* (John 2:19). John 10:17 bolsters this passage by stating, *"Therefore doth my Father love me, because I lay down my life, that I might take it again."* No, scribes and Pharisees, Jesus was not fidgeting but demonstrating an Eternal Truth as part of a Divine response. Respond He did! *"He that is without sin among you, let him first cast a stone at her."*

Jesus stooped down again and wrote again. His Work of Redemption always has a witness! Witness indeed! His death is our death, and His life is our life. The accusers felt a sense of conviction in their hearts and left "one by one." Like this woman, believers need to see that the whole Law, one by one is no longer present to accuse.

Jesus was Spirit-led! An obedient Son moving and speaking at Father's good pleasure. He was left alone with the woman. When He lifted up Himself again, there were no accusers. The same thing happened at Calvary! When He lifted up Himself, the woman or His Church has no accusers left. There was no man left to condemn her. The woman was so blessed to be delivered from her situation until she had to ask Jesus again whether there was no man to accuse her. His loving reply was *"neither do I condemn thee: go, and sin no more."* Jesus came giving a new commandment, *"That ye love one another; as I have loved you, that ye also love one another"* (John 13:34).

Grace is Part of God's Character

Psalm 103:8 "The LORD is merciful and gracious, slow to anger, and plenteous in mercy."

Psalm 111:4 "He hath made his wonderful works to be remembered: the LORD is gracious and full of compassion."

Psalm 116:5 "Gracious is the LORD, and righteous; yea, our God is merciful."

Psalm 145:8 "The LORD is gracious, and full of compassion; slow to anger, and of great mercy."

Chapter Fifteen

Grace Proves that God Remembers

Scripture Reading: Luke Chapter 1

The Gospel of Luke opens with the story of Zacharias and his wife, Elisabeth. It is of the essence to see them in their Scriptural context from the start. Luke 1:5 reads, *"There was in the days of Herod, the king of Judaea, a certain priest named Zacharias, of the course of Abia: and his wife was of the daughters of Aaron, and her name was Elisabeth. A certain priest whose name happens to translate remembered of Jehovah."* The name of his priestly course is critical to understanding the thought of God for us as well. *Abia* is the New Testament name for *Abijah* of the Old Testament. One may learn more about this priestly course from 1 Chronicles 24:10, where it was designated the eighth of the priestly courses. My father is Jah (Jehovah) is the meaning of Abijah.

Zacharias' wife was named Elisabeth or oath of God, and she was a daughter of Aaron, the Old Covenant High Priest whose name means *light bearer*. The couple was truly a match made in heaven. They were both righteous before God and walked before Him blameless. They picture priestly ministry in which the soul (the woman) is under the control of the spirit or inner man. On a broader note, they symbolize the Church submitted to Christ. There is not a more powerful combination under heaven.

Zacharias and Elisabeth had a situation that only a supernatural intervention could change. They were both well stricken in years, and Elisabeth was barren; however, through all the years they remained prayerful and faithful. On this priestly course, a heavenly messenger was about to visit them with great news. What a message the angel brought! *"Fear not, Zacharias: for thy prayer is heard; and thy wife Elisabeth shall bear thee a son, and thou shalt call his name John."* It is so refreshing that messages from heaven are so clear and contain all the required detail. Jehovah had remembered, and His oath remains sure. Their reward was a son who was to be called John or *Jehovah is a gracious giver!*

Let us look briefly at the attribute John or that which trumpets Jehovah as a gracious giver. Luke 1:14 states, *"And thou shalt have joy and gladness; and many shall rejoice at his birth."* Have you ever been sad about experiencing the grace of God? Instead, there is joy and gladness and praise and thanksgiving! Continuing with verse 15, *"For he shall be great in the sight of the Lord, and shall drink neither wine nor strong drink; and he shall be filled with the Holy Ghost, even from his mother's womb."* Goodness, gracious! A picture of a Nazarite wholly separated unto God for His purpose. Grace on arrival! And finally in verse 16, *"many of the children of Israel shall he turn to the Lord their God."* Souls numbering a number no man can number have come to altars for generations thanking God for His grace and turning their hearts unto him.

Zacharias was in awe regarding the words of Gabriel, the messenger, and questioned him from a natural perspective. A side lesson is in Zacharias' mistake for us all. One must understand that the spoken Word of God means that what He said is already so. Gabriel clarified his office and mission by saying, *"I am Gabriel, that stand in the presence of God; and am sent to speak unto thee, and to shew thee these glad tidings"* (Luke 1:19). This example is so important, and ministers of righteousness know to say what they have heard from the Presence of God, only.

Zacharias came forth from the temple speechless, and after the completion of the ministration of his priestly office, he returned home. He remained dumb until the fulfillment of the words of the angel. Doubt can never speak or witness for such glad tidings of eternal purpose; therefore, the silence was necessary. Such a seismic move of the Spirit requires prophecy or someone to speak grace to it rather than doubt.

Elisabeth conceived as Gabriel announced and did something intriguing. She hid her condition for five months. Astonishing! Five is the Bible number for grace. Elisabeth, the oath, said, *"Thus hath the Lord dealt with me in the days wherein he looked on me, to take away my reproach among men"* (Luke 1:25). Grace had replaced disgrace! No more shame! Now she was a walking expression of the faithfulness of God surrounded by grace fulfilling an eternal purpose.

Before John was born, the Holy Ghost filled this gift of grace. Mary, The Mother of Jesus, visited Elisabeth and John leaped in his mother's womb. Mary abode there for three months. Three is the Bible number for Resurrection and Divine Completion. The occasion was a thorough spiritual preparation, and John's birth was the fulfillment of time. A glance at Luke 1:58 shows the celebration of grace. All Elisabeth's neighbors and cousins heard how the Lord had shewed great mercy upon her, and they rejoiced with her! Zacharias' mouth opened, and he prophesied a past tense prophesy (Luke 1:73) even though Jesus had not been born which included the saying, *"The oath which he sware to our father, Abraham..."* Elisabeth or *oath*, well done for God remembered! When God says a thing, it is already so!

The gift of grace functions correctly under the right priestly order. It prepares the way for the Lord although it came by Him. Let a natural mind try to figure that point out. Eternity is encapsulated in grace and the Priestly Order of an Endless Life. This is the Order of Melchizedek which is the Order of our High Priest, Jesus Christ the Righteous. Dear reader, God has a plan of equal proportion for you as His grace takes you to your expected end.

Grace's Joy

Colossians 3:16 "Let the word of Christ dwell in you richly in all wisdom; teaching and admonishing one another in psalms and hymns and spiritual songs, singing with grace in your hearts to the Lord."

Galatians 1:15 "But when it pleased God, who separated me from my mother's womb, and called me by his grace,"

2 Timothy 1:9 "Who hath saved us, and called us with an holy calling, not according to our works, but according to his own purpose and grace, which was given us in Christ Jesus before the world began,"

CHAPTER SIXTEEN

WHEN GRACE BECOMES THANKSGIVING

There are some occasions in Scripture where the word "thanks" references the word "grace" instead. A few instances are cited and expounded upon herein. First, The Apostle Paul noticeably uses thanks as grace in his epistles to the Corinthians. In his first epistle to that church, he said, *"But thanks be to God, which giveth us the victory through our Lord Jesus Christ"* (1 Corinthians 15:57). The word *thanks* expressed for the victory given through Jesus Christ is the same Greek word for *"grace"* which is charis!

The verses preceding contain a mystery (1 Corinthians 15: 50-55). The *mystery* or hidden truth is to the natural man but revealed to the man with a renewed spirit. The mystery is *"We shall not all sleep, but we shall all be changed"* (1 Corinthians 15:51). Interestingly, the term *sleep* is used instead of die. Always be mindful that to Resurrection and Life (Jesus) death is merely *sleeping* (John 11:25). Case in point, Lazarus was dead, but Jesus, the Resurrection, and the Life said He was going to wake him out of *sleep*.

All shall be changed! A Divine exchange will take place. In other words, one thing for another or incorruption for corruption. What a transformation! The Apostle Paul went on to describe the process in verse 52. *"In a moment, in the twinkling of an eye, at the last trump: for the trumpet shall sound, and the dead shall be raised incorruptible, and we shall be changed."* As we become the essence of grace, It becomes gratitude for us. While a *mo-*

ment does speak to a moment in time like most would comprehend, there is a far reaching spiritual meaning to it also. A *moment* is that which *cannot cut in two, or divided, indivisible* according to Strong's Exhaustive Concordance. It is the Greek word *atomos* where our word atom, the basic unit of a chemical element, is derived.

Here is a precise time where a promise Jesus made is in force. Of the Holy Spirit, He said, *"He shall glorify me: for he shall receive of mine, and shall shew it unto you"* (John 16:14). Grace is the means for putting Jesus on full display. Pray that God gives us ears to hear the Voice of the Holy Spirit.

Once we experience our spiritual moment or atomos, there will be nothing left of us. Only Christ will remain. Self-righteousness pulverized! Carnality crushed! Here we have the removal of the old and the establishing of the new. The Apostle Paul understood clearly when he testified, *"I am crucified with Christ: nevertheless I live; yet not I, <u>but Christ liveth in me</u>: and the life which I now live in the flesh I live by the faith of the Son of God, who loved me, and gave himself for me"* (Galatians 2:20). Christ Jesus on display through His Body changes grace to thanksgiving. Grace and truth are consummated within.

Another place where grace is translated thanks is found in 2 Corinthians 2:14 which states, *"Now thanks be unto God, which always causeth us to triumph in Christ, and maketh manifest the savour of his knowledge by us in every place."* Our location or position in Christ always causes us to triumph! This verse contains the only usage of the word *triumph* in the New Testament. Perhaps it includes a powerful truth that merits intense exploration. Not only is there triumph or victory, but the celebration thereof is a unit of the triumph. An integral part of the triumph. The celebration is not a subsequent event but takes place within the triumph. That is a different tone altogether. Not a hand and a glove but a hand in glove!

For some, this point will underscore the importance of praise! Praise and triumph are simultaneous in the life of the believer because they are one and the same spiritually. The Psalmist cried out, *"Save us, O LORD our God, and gather us from among the heathen, to give thanks unto thy holy name, and to triumph in thy praise"* (Psalm 106:47). The triumph is in the praise! It is worth repeating that we are saved and separated unto God to give thanks and triumph in His praise.

The second part of 2 Corinthians 2:15, above also shows thanksgiving to God for *making manifest the savour of His knowledge by us in every place.* Therefore verse 14 is worthy of dissection for the enjoyment of every holy morsel. Knowledge of God has a fragrance that He makes prominent through us in every place. A powerful testimony to this truth happened in the early years of our ministry. There was a couple, and the wife attended regularly, but her husband did not. He decided to come with her one Sunday and God demonstrated this exact verse in a literal yet spiritually penetrating manner. The wife later reported that her husband asked whether or not we burned incense in the church which we never have. He smelled a God-sent fragrance as The Word went forth in power. It is extraordinary to watch God put His Signature on His Work. In his greeting, The Apostle Peter acknowledged that grace and peace are multiplied through the knowledge of God and of Jesus Christ our Lord (2 Peter 1:2), and He manifests this knowledge through us! Thank You, Heavenly Father!

To further put 2 Corinthians 2:15 in context, The Apostle Paul went on the point out, "For we are unto God a sweet savor of Christ, in them that are saved, and in them that perish." Astonishing! Notice what ministering Christ and His Work of Redemption does. The Spirit of the Word is indeed sharper than any two-edged sword. Single-handedly, the Word divides asunder between soul and spirit and of the joints and marrow and is a discerner of the thoughts and intents of the heart. Power! God changes not, and He loves everyone; however, He needs acceptance. There is a warning to it all in verse 16. *"To the one we are the savor of death unto death; and to the other the savor of life unto life."* This Divine Effect has worked flawlessly in our ministry for 23 years and will continue as long as Christ ministers. It is a sobering and humbling point that we are a sweet savor or fragrance of Christ. How glorious that the very Christ Himself is moving and ministering to His people everywhere who are sincere and will not corrupt His Word (2 Corinthians 2:15-17).

Thanks and *grace* used interchangeably by a son of God indicates maturity in Christ. This maturity is not a by-and-by thing at all. If going on to maturity was not meant for our time here on the earth, the Scriptures would not have declared so. Ephesians 4:11-13 is worth injecting here to seal that thought. *"And he gave some, apostles; and some, prophets; and some, evangelists; and some, pastors and teachers; For the perfecting of the saints, for the work of the ministry, for the edifying of the body of Christ: Till we all come in the unity of the faith, and of the knowledge of the Son of God, unto a perfect man, unto the measure of the stature of the fullness of Christ:"*

These ministries were given by Jesus when He ascended on high. Many have taken the ministries as titles unto themselves to lord over the people of God. The ministries were given *"till."* The concept of "till" in the Bible is not always and forever! If ministry is not bringing the Body unto the measure of the stature of the fullness of Christ, then it is not given by Christ. Leading people to Jesus is a blessed start, but there should be ministry taking those same individuals into His Fullness.

The word *"thanks"* is used in place of the word grace again in 2 Corinthians 9:15 which says, *"Thanks be unto God for his unspeakable gift."* How would one consider something unspeakable unless he has experienced it? What Divine emphasis we find when the Effect of the Christ is manifest! Just Jesus! The full description of the gift becomes such that only heaven can utter it. In this realm sufficient words elude us, but we often settle for expressions such as *unspeakable, indescribable, inexpressible, or too wonderful for words!*

Still, there is one expression that God receives as enough, and that is *thanks*. When grace has accomplished Its mission, one can only say thanks and worship God. This train of thought is probably a reason Scripture occasionally uses *thanks* alternately with *grace*. As an additional note, thanksgiving is included in worship in heaven before the Throne (Revelation 7:12).

During an occasion in Jesus' earthly ministry (Luke 17:12-19), He healed ten lepers. They cried out to Jesus for mercy, He spoke, and as they obeyed, they received healing. According to custom, he told them, "Go show themselves to the priest, and as they went, they were cleansed." One of the lepers returned and gave *thanks*. To highlight what *thanksgiving* means to God, notice Jesus' response. *"Were there not ten cleansed? But where are the nine?"* Only one, who happened to be a Samaritan or stranger, returned on his face to give glory to God. Giving thanks is giving glory!

A magnificent spiritual event occurred in this miracle other than the natural manifestation of healing. Those lepers who went on their way got their release from a Levitical priestly order. That order cannot bring that which is perfect. The leper that returned to Jesus got his release from a Melchizedek Priest after the Order of an Endless Life. Jesus told him to arise and go his way. Notice Jesus did not say run and catch up to those going to the priests. By returning to give thanks, this man's faith made him whole or clean through the word spoken by Jesus (John 15:3). Thanksgiving through faith acknowledged Jesus and grace responded in an eternal way.

Grace Edifies

1 Corinthians 3:10 "According to the grace of God which is given unto me, as a wise masterbuilder, I have laid the foundation, and another buildeth thereon. But let every man take heed how he buildeth thereupon."

2 Corinthians 8: 7 "Therefore, as ye abound in every thing, in faith, and utterance, and knowledge, and in all diligence, and in your love to us, see that ye abound in this grace also."

Colossians 1:5-6 "For the hope which is laid up for you in heaven, whereof ye heard before in the word of the truth of the gospel; Which is come unto you, as it is in all the world; and bringeth forth fruit, as it doth also in you, since the day ye heard of it, and knew the grace of God in truth:"

Ephesians 4:7 "But unto every one of us is given grace according to the measure of the gift of Christ."

2 Thessalonians 1:12 "That the name of our Lord Jesus Christ may be glorified in you, and ye in him, according to the grace of our God and the Lord Jesus Christ."

1 Peter 1:13 "Wherefore gird up the loins of your mind, be sober, and hope to the end for the grace that is to be brought unto you at the revelation of Jesus Christ;"

Chapter Seventeen

A Preposition Changed My Life Forever

"But when it pleased God, who separated me from my mother›s womb, and called me by His grace, <u>To reveal His Son in me,</u> that I might preach Him among the heathen; immediately I conferred not with flesh and blood: Neither went I up to Jerusalem to them which were apostles before me; but I went into Arabia, and returned again unto Damascus." Galatians 1:15-17

Early on my journey, I expected Christ to reveal himself <u>to</u> me. I repeat, <u>to</u> me. My wrong interpretation of the preposition "in" used by the Apostle Paul in the above Scripture robbed me of enjoying my Inheritance in Christ Jesus for many years. I sought my Beloved in all the wrong, sensual places under the guise of ministry. Praise God for restoration. Webster defines a preposition as follows: *"In grammar, a word usually put before another to express some relation or quality, action or motion to or from the thing specified; as medicines, salutary to health; music agreeable to the ear; virtue is valued for its excellence; a man is riding to Oxford from London."* Elementary but hopefully, this grammatical refresher will help the reader better understand my previous dilemma.

When the Apostle Paul stated that it pleased God to reveal His Son in him, my brain processed the preposition «to» instead of «in.» I am not alone in this misinterpretation. One can readily observe the exorbitant amount of stimulus that is inundating many places in ministries such as props, drama, big screens, whether groups are large or small, and other dynamic media, and see that the masses expect something to be revealed <u>to</u> them instead of <u>in</u> them. I am forever grateful to the Spirit of Truth for calling my attention to the error of my thinking.

According to the New Covenant, there is a mystery hidden from the ages *which is Christ in you the hope of glory* (Colossians 1:27). The average person is not expecting Christ to reveal Himself from within them. Religion has meticulously put too much space between them and their loving Father and His Christ. It is almost as though one has never read Jesus' prayer in the Book of John. "<u>I in them</u>, and thou in me, that they may be made perfect in one; and that the world may know that thou hast sent me, and hast loved them, as thou hast loved me. And I have declared unto them thy name, and will declare it: that the love wherewith thou hast loved me may be in them, and I in them" (John 17:23, 26).

The Apostle Paul met the Resurrected Christ, our Blessed Lord, instead of another's version of Him. In Paul's separation, he learned the uninhibited Power of God unleashed in the Lord's obedience unto death. In their initial meeting, Paul (Saul) received greeting with the question from the Lord (Acts 9:4), *"Saul, Saul, why persecutest thou, Me?"* The Lord Jesus and His Body had become One. With Paul's subsequent name change came a new creation nature. He learned that Love neither excluded nor failed anyone.

The Apostle Paul must have been indelibly impressed with the wonderful deliverance at Ananias' house. Ananias means grace. It was at "grace's house" that he learned that God's unmerited favor was available to aid instead of accuse. His eyes came open by the Spirit, and the Divine Transaction of the Cross began to work <u>in</u> him. He discerned that we were crucified with Christ yet lived (Romans 6:6; Galatians 2:20; Galatians 6:14). Only now, we are no longer living, but Christ now lives in us! He understood that we died with Christ, and the old man with his corrupt nature was buried with Him (Romans 6:4,8; Colossians 3:3). When reminded of his dialog with the Divine Light and Its Voice on the road to Damascus, he engaged his new ability to fathom the result of the quickening Power of God. In addition to that, as a new creation after the Spirit, he boldly declared that we were quickened together with Christ (Ephesians 2:5; Colossians 2:13). One holy conversation with the Resurrected Christ and Paul received an unwarranted invite into a whole new realm of life in the Spirit.

Although others in the Apostle Paul's company when he was on the road to Damascus saw the Light, they could not hear the Voice. Paul became intimately familiar with the simplicity in Christ and how the mind can be corrupted from it as the serpent beguiled Eve. He warned that there is another gospel out there that produces another spirit (2 Corinthians 11). His separation culminated in his realization that we were raised and seated together with Christ in heavenly places (Colossians 3:1; Ephesians 2:6). It is so gloriously fulfilling to realize that God always lands us in a position of rest with Himself.

One of the most feared Books in the Bible is The Revelation of Jesus Christ. That amazes me seeing that the first Words of the Book are, *"The Revelation of Jesus Christ, which God gave unto him, to shew unto his servants things which must shortly come to pass..."* (Revelation 1:1). Why should the unveiling or uncovering of Jesus Christ be a fearful thing for the believer? This glorious Book describes our Lord and His Finished Work in signs and language of the Spirit. Allow Him to demonstrate His Work in us and watch Him begin to flow out of us. It is a quick work that indeed comes to pass from within us shortly after we truly believe! What fear? *"For ye are dead, and your life is hid with Christ in God"* (Colossians 3:3). It pleases God to reveal His Son in us!

Grace's Location

2 Timothy 2:1 "Thou therefore, my son, be strong in the grace that is in Christ Jesus."

Hebrews 4:16 "Let us therefore come boldly unto the throne of grace, that we may obtain mercy, and find grace to help in time of need."

CHAPTER EIGHTEEN

FRUSTRATING THE WORK OF GRACE

"I do not frustrate the grace of God: for if righteousness come by the law, then Christ is dead in vain." Galatians 2:21

The Old Testament contains a zoomed picture that captures the essence of the thought of this chapter. In the Book of Ezra, Chapter 4, the children of the Babylonian captivity were building the temple unto God. Our focus is on the first five verses of Ezra Chapter 4, and the reader is highly encouraged to privately study Ezra and Nehemiah for a complete understanding of what happened during a time of the restoration of the temple. Although a shadow of the Truth, a careful study of their time will reveal many truths that will benefit the believer today. There are too many treasures of truth to cite here, but examples abound.

Noteworthy is the fact that, although King Cyrus released the Jews from captivity, some chose to stay. One can relate that example to present day conditions in some places. People are free but will not walk in the liberty afforded them in Christ. Although Jesus has made a way into the holiest of all through His Flesh, many choose to stay in the captivity of sin or the bondage of the world system. Those who were faithful and willing came out of Babylon (confusion) to resume the work of the Lord God. Their purpose was frustrated, and a sea of knowledge and insight can be gained from their experience.

To frustrate means to break or make void. We have a tenacious adversary but do not be alarmed. Despite his persistence, faith keeps the believer above and ahead of his adversary because of his position in Christ. Think about the purpose of something adversarial. It causes resistance. Guess what? So, does physical exercise. Ever notice people who work out regularly? It is obvious. They are toned and lean and even glow. My husband, Bishop Paul Bynum, Sr., is a perfect example. A physically and spiritually fit son of God. God has a purpose in all things, and our adversaries are simply means for strengthening us spiritually at our Father's good pleasure. The harder they work, the stronger we get. The discomfort is temporary. The result is that our faith increases, and we become strong and wise in Christ.

Read carefully the situation of Ezra 4:1-5.

> [1] Now when the adversaries of Judah and Benjamin heard that the children of the captivity builded the temple unto the LORD God of Israel; [2] Then they came to Zerubbabel, and to the chief of the fathers, and said unto them, Let us build with you: for we seek your God, as ye do; and we do sacrifice unto him since the days of Esarhaddon king of Assur, which brought us up hither. [3] But Zerubbabel, and Jeshua, and the rest of the chief of the fathers of Israel, said unto them, Ye have nothing to do with us to build an house unto our God; but we ourselves together will build unto the LORD God of Israel, as king Cyrus the king of Persia hath commanded us. [4] Then the people of the land weakened the hands of the people of Judah, and troubled them in building, [5] And hired counsellors against them, to frustrate their purpose, all the days of Cyrus king of Persia, even until the reign of Darius king of Persia.

When Law is present while Grace's multifaceted ministry is ongoing, the adversaries of Judah and Benjamin are bound to show up under the guise of helpers. These people symbolize the real spiritual deal. Jesus is the Lion of the Tribe of Judah and Benjamin's name means son of the right hand. Jesus sits at the right Hand of God, and we are in Him (Ephesians 2:6). Flesh always vies for a place in the things of God alongside His sons. *"Let us build with you for we seek your God as ye do."* Flesh under the power of Law will always have a history to rehearse in the ears of those moving in the power of God's grace on their spiritual journey in Christ.

Notice, the adversaries' words, *"We do sacrifice unto him since the days of Esarhaddon king of Assur, which brought us up hither."*

Praise God for Zerubbabel and Jeshua and the rest of the fathers of Israel! They represent the King/Priest Ministry of the Lord Jesus Christ and mature sons in Him. Such can discern and will not allow that which is carnal to work alongside them in the things of God. They understand that they represent the Spiritual Kingdom of God, precisely, and the adversary has no part in it. Not one inch of place is handed over because it will lead to a foothold, and consequently, mixture and defeat. *"Ye have nothing to do with us to build an house unto our God."* God will have a pure ministry in this earth unto Himself. Some ministries are allying with the world, but there are those of us who understand that it is in Christ Jesus only that we live, move and have our very being. We understand that by His shed Blood, He has made us kings and priests unto God and His Father (Revelation 1:6), and we are His temple.

Ezra 4:4-5 above shows plainly the opposition that will come when God has a people unto Himself in purity and power. These Scriptures are not to discourage believers but rather to encourage. Just focus on the end of the matter which is the Restoration we already have in Christ Jesus! There will be those who will do all they can to weaken the hands. Remember, the term to consecrate means to fill the hands. There will be those who will try to convince sons that they are not set apart for God's purpose in order to hinder their praise. Notice it was the hands of Judah also known as praise. There will also be those who will try to terrify the "builders" and make them fearful and confused. The adversary does not want Babylon which means confusion to lose its grip. They will even go to great lengths to oppose by hiring counselors against them. Today such counselors are hirelings in pulpits and other places speaking anything but Truth which frustrates the purpose.

Now let us go to our New Testament example. The Apostle Paul said to the Church at Galatia, *"I do not frustrate the grace of God: for if righteousness come by the law, then Christ is dead in vain"* (Galatians 2:21). His words are quite succinct. The frustration of grace comes when one believes the Law can justify him. To that person, Christ died in vain. The Cross of Christ is the one Transaction that restored God's people unto Himself building a spiritual house not made with man's hands! Not as the house seen in Ezra but the Building of God with Christ Himself the Cornerstone! Anyone coming against this Stone will stumble! This Stone, Christ Jesus, has been made unto God's people, wisdom, righteousness, sanctification and redemption (1 Corinthians 1:30). What could man possibly need physically or spiritually that he cannot find in Christ?

The Apostle Paul had already declared in the preceding verse Galatians 2:20, *"I am crucified with Christ: nevertheless I live; yet not I, but Christ liveth in me: and the life which I now live in the flesh I live by the faith of the Son of God, who loved me, and gave himself for me."* If a believer does not have an understanding of this one verse, he will fall prey to the mixture of carnality and spirituality every time. Self-righteousness will represent a badge of honor and grace will have zero room to work in that life. Grace moves in the Power of the Resurrected Christ. The Apostle Paul understood that if the Law justifies one, *"Christ becomes no effect unto him, and he is fallen from grace"* (Galatians 5:4). Frustrate the grace of God and be frustrated with God.

Grace's Edification

1 Corinthians 3:10 "According to the grace of God which is given unto me, as a wise masterbuilder, I have laid the foundation, and another buildeth thereon. But let every man take heed how he buildeth thereupon."

2 Corinthians 8: 7 "Therefore, as ye abound in every thing, in faith, and utterance, and knowledge, and in all diligence, and in your love to us, see that ye abound in this grace also."

Colossians 1:5-6 "For the hope which is laid up for you in heaven, whereof ye heard before in the word of the truth of the gospel; Which is come unto you, as it is in all the world; and bringeth forth fruit, as it doth also in you, since the day ye heard of it, and knew the grace of God in truth:"

Ephesians 4:7 "But unto every one of us is given grace according to the measure of the gift of Christ."

2 Thessalonians 1:12 "That the name of our Lord Jesus Christ may be glorified in you, and ye in him, according to the grace of our God and the Lord Jesus Christ."

1 Peter 1:13 "Wherefore gird up the loins of your mind, be sober, and hope to the end for the grace that is to be brought unto you at the revelation of Jesus Christ;"

Chapter Nineteen

Grace Writes Love Songs About Jesus

Early in ministry, I began to notice many inspirational songs affected the soul, but not many reached the spirit. Certainly, there are myriads of talented and anointed singers, musicians, and songwriters in the Kingdom, known and unknown, sung and unsung. As we ascend in the Lord Jesus Christ, the melodies and words come to us, and we give them back to the Lord. Following are some lyrics received along this blessed journey. They represent a mother lode of praises given to us by ***grace***. Their melodies are supremely heavenly, and we look forward to sharing them with the Body.

BY YOUR GRACE

©2004 Written and arranged by Carolyn P. Bynum

Verse 1

Lord, when You tell me what to do,

I need only look to You,

And it's already done.

Your Wisdom is my Light;

Your Spirit is my sight;

I Do Not Frustrate God's Grace

The Victory's won

In Christ the Son!

Chorus: No matter how I try;

I can't exhaust this great Supply.

As I run this race,

I'm powered by Your Grace!

Verse 2

My life is set apart

Since You came into my heart.

Faith is the key!

As You live Your Life through me

I can see I've truly been set free,

Far above every enemy.

Chorus: No matter how I try;

I can't exhaust this great Supply.

As I run this race,

I'm powered by Your Grace!

WE ARE WORDS FROM GOD!

©2009 Written and arranged by Carolyn P. Bynum

We are words from God,

Each a blessed and needed part;

A holy message from above.

The full expression of His mercy and His grace;

Sent from Father's heart with all His love.

We are words from God,

Incomplete without each other;

Established in power and pure.

We must be a reflection of our one Foundation;

Forever settled in heaven; Sure.

We are words from God,

Always a faithful saying;

Led by His Spirit alone.

Our lives must speak a Word in every situation;

A Voice that flows out of His Throne.

We are words from God,

That will never leave a question;

Revealing the fullness of His Son.

When we all come together, it will be so very lovely;

Father and His children all in One.

Bridge: We're not here on our own.

We're sent from Father's heart with all His love!

<u>HIS WORD!</u>

©2009 Written and arranged by Carolyn P. Bynum

God said it!

He meant it!

He'll do it!

Just as He said He would!

His Word is

The only Thing

That is magnified

Above His Precious, Holy Name!

No matter what trial or test.

Receive of God's very best!

Keep your mind on Who's Faithful and True!

He'll surely, surely come through for you!

Just believe it!

Never doubt it!

Keep on waiting

You'll see that He's so very near!

The Word became Flesh

Now flesh becomes Word.

Keep on watching;

In your life He will appear!

You're not merely here just by chance.

You've got an Inheritance!

Keep your mind on what He's promised to do.

He'll surely, surely come through for you!

Not matter what the circumstance,

Christ is your Inheritance!

Keep your mind on what He's promised to do.

He'll surely, surely come through for you!

HEAVEN

©2012 Written and arranged by Carolyn P. Bynum

I heard so much about heaven,

A place so bright and fair.

When I asked Jesus to live and rule in my heart,

I knew at once I was seated with Him there!

All that comes down from heaven

Will testify of our Lord

Fire to purify

Or glorify

All Fulfilling God's Holy Word!

I heard so much about heaven

Where all mysteries are known in the Son.

When Father filled me with His Holy Spirit,

I knew at once we were joined as one!

All that comes down from heaven

Will testify of our Lord

Angels descend and ascend

Have a message of Love with no end

All Fulfilling God's Holy Word

I heard so much about heaven

Where a city built and made by God doth abide

When I saw Christ being revealed from within His Church,

I knew at once this City was His Purchased Bride!

All that comes down from heaven

Will testify of our Lord!

In the Fullness of His Holy Name

Christ and heaven are both the same!

All things fulfilled by God's Holy Word!

ZION

(©2007 Written & arranged by the Holy Spirit through

Carolyn P. Bynum)

Ye are come unto Mt. Zion.

Your spirit has come home.

Joined to the Lord eternally;

Just men made perfect, fully free.

You know that you're at Zion

I Do Not Frustrate God's Grace

Because His Holy Presence is your Home!

Beautiful for situation;

Joy of all the earth.

It's where our God has set His King.

Listen to His praises ring!

You know that you're at Zion

Because His Holy Presence is your Home!

Source of strength and salvation.

There's a precious Corner Stone.

This and that man were born in her;

The Highest has established her!

You know that you're at Zion

Because His Holy Presence is your Home!

Now that you're at Zion

In Christ, the race is won.

All who appear before His Face

Are sons of Spirit, saved by grace.

You know that you're at Zion

Because His Holy Presence is your Home!

ALL HAIL! THE KING IS HERE!

©2014 Written and arranged by Carolyn P. Bynum

All Hail! The King is here!

All Hail! The King is here!

We have been waiting,

Our joy is full when You appear!

Humbly waiting,

There is peace and love when you are near.

On us descend, Dear Lord,

Stay and abide within.

We are your temple, and we are your dwelling place.

All Hail! The King is here!

All Hail! The King is here!

We have been waiting,

Our joy is full when You appear

Humbly waiting,

There is perfect love no doubt or fear,

Your Power endued, Dear Lord,

Our strength is now renewed.

We are your temple, and we are your dwelling place.

A LIFE THAT IS HIGHER

©2004 Written and arranged by Carolyn P. Bynum

There is a Life that is higher!

It's full of God's grace and power.

There is a Life where no darkness

Can ever prevail!

There is a Life in Christ Jesus, our Lord

Just as it says in His Word.

And It's full of Light

Where Love can never fail.

Chapter Twenty

One of Many Testimonies of Grace

In 1998, a true servant of God spoke into my life by the Holy Spirit. He said that "God is strategically planting houses all over this nation that seem like they are in the day of small things. However, I hear the Lord saying, do not despise the day of little things and don't let men despise your youth. When I say that I'm talking about the age of not so much as your physical being, but the ministry that is there. I hear the Lord saying that He's planting and preparing because He's got to get barns before He can bring in a harvest. Hallelujah! I hear the Lord saying that you've been in a season and a time of preparation. Even though there is like a handful, I hear the Lord saying that He's going to cause there to be people that you are going to get their attention, and they're going to come. As you just establish my house after the Pattern, I show you watch and see if I won't do the work of bringing you the people. They will include not just the weird and outcast, and the ones that are just fly-by-night, here today and gone tomorrow, but stable people. Quality individuals and people that are going to give a platform for the Word of the Lord to spread all over. I hear the Lord saying that the territory is the Southwest and all over that region. There is just going to be a multiplication as the Lord begins to bring multiplication in your house, Hallelujah! I see God releasing something in that region like a new sun rising. Isn't there something in Phoenix about the sun? I hear the Lord saying there's a new Sun about to arise. Hallelujah! A new Sun is about to rise, and a new light is going to break forth. Darkness now rebuked, Hallelujah!

Amen! Therefore, changes are coming in that region. In the Name of Jesus, we just release that. Thank You, Lord, God."

At the time, our ministry was in its infancy (only four years old) and vibrant with activities. Immediately, mental pictures formed of building a larger building with even more people and continuing to do what we were already doing. After all, we were preaching the Gospel. I knew that the message was from God, and He cannot lie. The problem was that I tailored God's promise to my limited concept. Despite the powerful teaching anointing God had entrusted to me, I foolishly tried to frame the infinite Thought of God within my little setting.

People were accommodating as long as they were "busy." Auxiliaries in the ministry began to take on their own personalities. As the Word continued to come in power, I noticed some in leadership positions had difficulty focusing. Some began to rush out of service to take part in other "activities" or personal fellowships, although the Spirit was still moving. The Spirit opened my eyes to many subtle tactics of the enemy. Some leaders began to use the children's ministry as a means to escape from the power of the Word. I focused on preaching the Gospel. No matter how people acted, I preached Christ and Him crucified. Open rebellion among leadership ensued.

Praise God for the prophetic anointing upon my husband, Paul. We had a banquet with the theme, "Walking in the Spirit." While attending the dinner, my husband heard God say to him, *"Woe to the man who does not receive this woman."* By the Spirit, both my husband and I began to see God was calling this ministry unto Himself. We are not just "another ministry" but an integral part of His Bride. About a year after that banquet we were growing by the power of the Spirit Who was ministering Christ on levels we had never dreamed. My husband had the deacons remove the banquet banner that read "Walking in the Spirit" from storage and place it on permanent display before the people. God began to magnify His presence in our midst and demonstrate His power as we turned to Him with all our hearts. As I came to see all things Christ-centered and how self-effort was futile, He began to minister with such power through me that it became necessary for me to listen to every recording to capture all God said. Rebellious hearts became increasingly more restless and distracting.

God revealed the enemy working through some of the most gifted and talented people in the ministry to my husband and me in dreams and visions. Once we were vacationing, my husband and I had nearly identical dreams concerning an individual who later turned against the ministry. I was stunned as I saw the spirit of jealousy upon ones who pretended to be closest. A couple of "ministers" would cry continually as the Word came forth, but by the Holy Spirit, I could see these were not tears of joy and praise. We witnessed a scream from a realm so dark a horror movie director would have been awed by it. I knew the power of Christ was with us in full force. Demons were no longer terrorizing but now in terror. Many who turned against us were the very ones who never seemed able to do enough for us. We asked those leaving the ministry what we had done to offend them? Not one person could give us a specific reason for leaving. It is a truth; God's people will never be taken by surprise when we walk in the power of His Spirit. Witches (yes, plural), planted by Satan, began to cry out especially during praise and worship and the preaching of the Cross of Christ. On two separate occasions, women, who were used of the devil to come against the ministry, actually ran from the sanctuary screaming. Surprisingly, even some "seasoned warriors" thought they were caught up in the "spirit." *"He that hath an ear let him hear."*

The work of the enemy manifested through leaders as constant strife and division. One person worked tirelessly to try to isolate my family and me from every person in the ministry. People actually underestimated the Consuming Fire that God is. The power of God is in the preaching of the Gospel! The fallen man cannot stand the heat and will definitely "get out of the kitchen." *"They went out from us, but they were not of us; for if they had been of us, they would no doubt have continued with us: but they went out, that they might be made manifest that they were not all of us." (1 John 2:19).*

We are either of Christ or the first man, Adam. Many believe the Antichrist is a natural person raised up from the earth, but let me assure every reader, the spirit of the antichrist is not what many have been led to believe. Anyone or anything that opposes our Beloved Christ is the antiChrist. When the fallen man continually rebels against Christ, people become blind to the choke-hold with which wickedness has them bound. Surely, the Light of Christ rebukes the kingdom of darkness. The tactic was to destroy the Seed. Instead, there was an ejection of the wicked. We are still standing in the power of God's might.

Many other things happened; however, it is not my intention to sensationalize the reader's attention and draw one away from God's powerful dealings with us. One must stay in the Spirit. We became the "poison" and outcasts of the community for many. Many pastors shunned us. Others who have known us for years refused to reach out to us. We stayed focused on the Pattern, Jesus Christ. Although I simply preached the Finished Work of Christ, I was labeled a charlatan and heretic. A concerted effort to prevent others from attending was undertaken by some who left. People judged us without even knowing us. We had tirelessly sown into lives of many who walked away without a second thought. There were precisely five *(or a handful)* of us left. *A stable people!* Great Grace! Truly, amazing grace!

When we felt like giving up, the Lord encouraged us to stand. One day my husband was in our back yard, and the Lord spoke to him. He came inside and told me, "I just heard God say, 'Just stand!'" Those words were confirmed a few months later through our beloved Pastor, Gary Garner, Ascension Life Ministries, Danville, Arkansas who has now transitioned to glory. While imparting through the laying on of hands and praying for us, Pastor Garner said by the Spirit, *"No matter how many people leave your church, you just stand!"* God confirmed His Word to my husband. Just stand! His grace is truly sufficient.

We are still standing because Christ is standing in us. What a *season of preparation!* The season is for our benefit. My grandmother used to say, "God is too wise to make a mistake." The peace that kept us through it all was the powerful Presence of God. His Presence intensified more and more as the purging continued. His ways are past finding out! His presence is enough, and His grace is sufficient indeed. His strength is made perfect in weakness. Praise God for His wonderful grace!

We thank our Heavenly Father for the personal lessons learned, and we continue learning daily. Most importantly, we learned to wait on the Lord and to depend wholly upon Him. We are continually learning the power of walking in the Spirit. There is a place where Christ becomes our very life. God has opened heaven to us and has shown us great and mighty things in His Son. We learned through this Divine season of preparation that the *letter killeth but the Spirit giveth life.* Those in tradition live by the letter, but the Bride lives by the Spirit. What a life we have in the Son! We watched God as He proceeded to do what He said He would do, precisely; once the removal of "self." People wanted to see His glory. His glory appeared and revealed the hearts of men. Many faded and fainted. His faithful followers remained.

There was no intention for the message of the Christ in this ministry meant for confinement to a local assembly. This ministry is truly a *"platform for the Word of God to spread."* We are reaching not only our local region but this country and many parts of the world as well. Scripture states that God hideth His power. Televised ministry is not the only effective avenue to spread the Word of God. It is likely that many of you are more effective in the kingdom of God right now in your waiting season than many with daily television programs. In fact, ministries that have had the most profound impact on my life and ministry were not televangelists. God strategically placed the most truly spiritual ministries in my path. By stealth, God is moving in His true church, and we (His True Church) all know it.

Before closing, I must share one final point that may help the reader. Many times, people are hurting physically, emotionally or spiritually. They seek immediate relief. Many gather unto "prophetic conferences" to get a personal prophecy. They want help, and they want it now. Revelation 19:10 reads in part, *"the testimony of Jesus is the spirit of prophecy."* He is the best Word one will ever receive. Once you receive Him, you will start to express Him. In that expression, material things start to lose their luster and appeal. Every reader is encouraged to go into every situation seeking Christ. Cast down every lofty thing that exalts itself above the knowledge of Him. If He is not in the situation, you should not be there.

Early in ministry, I was allied with a non-denominational group that was a denomination in itself. The leader's style was abrasive and ineffective. When he ministered, there was very little Word and lots of "personal prophecy." By the Spirit, I came to recognize this style as mere religion coupled with soul power paraded as Gospel truth. Take heed when the Bible speaks of lying wonders for it is very true. What a crowd it draws! Many people fell for the seduction and were held captive while looking for help apart from Christ. The "prophecies" always centered on material things or personal "words" instead of Christ. Everything was "prophesied" from millions of dollars to kingdoms themselves. Material things took higher priority which only Christ deserves. From first-hand experience, be warned that the Word of God is true when it says, "no man can serve two masters."

Through it all, the most powerful and accurate prophecies came from true servants of God who simply encouraged the ministry with the Finished Work and simplicity of Christ. They are the prophecies that came to pass and are still coming to pass for they testify of my Beloved, the Christ of God, thereby we know they are true. Like Abraham, we must meet Melchizedek before we meet the king of Sodom. Melchizedek served Abraham "bread and wine" which pictures Christ in Redemption. He later met the King of Sodom who offered him natural riches. Abraham wisely declined the king saying that no man will say that a man made him rich. Armed with Redemptive power one will recognize the true from the false immediately. Many seek riches and miss their Visitation because they have not met the Priest after the Order of an Endless Life. His Name is Jesus! Wealth comes embodied in Christ, and He is a Treasure indeed! I praise and thank God for taking care of His Church, this ministry, my family and me. May the eternal blessings in Christ Jesus be upon every reader!

Grace's Benediction

Romans 16:24 "The grace of our Lord Jesus Christ be with you all. Amen."

2 Corinthians 13:14 "The grace of the Lord Jesus Christ, and the love of God, and the communion of the Holy Ghost, be with you all. Amen."

Ephesians 6: 24 "Grace **be** *with all them that love our Lord Jesus Christ in sincerity. Amen."*

Galatians 6:18 "Brethren, the grace of our Lord Jesus Christ be with your spirit. Amen."

2 Peter 3:18 "But grow in grace, and in the knowledge of our Lord and Saviour Jesus Christ. To him be glory both now and for ever. Amen."

Hebrews 13:25 "Grace **be** *with you all. Amen."*

Philemon 1:25 "The grace of our Lord Jesus Christ **be** *with your spirit. Amen."*

2 Timothy 4:22 "The Lord Jesus Christ **be** *with thy spirit. Grace* **be** *with you. Amen."*

Revelation 22:21 "The grace of our Lord Jesus Christ be with you all. Amen."

About the Author

Carolyn P. Bynum is the founder and pastor of Restoration Christian Ministries Center, Sierra Vista, Arizona. Pastor Bynum is an anointed teacher sent to the Body of Christ. She has been ministering for more than two decades. Her audio and video ministry reach most of the USA and several other nations. Her local radio outreach has blessed the local community and outlying areas for more than 20 years. She is a Spirit-filled, ordained minister and noted conference speaker. Pastor Bynum is also a musician, lyricist, and arranger who has written numerous praise and worship songs. She served 21 years of honorable active military service in the Army and retired as a Chief Warrant Officer Three with numerous decorations, commendations and citations from both and war and peacetime. She has Bachelor's Degree in Behavioral Science from Western International University and a Master's Degree in Counseling from Chapman University. Pastor Bynum wants the world to know that, like the Apostle Paul, the Gospel she preaches is not of man neither was she taught it, but it pleased God to reveal His Son, Jesus Christ in her. Her vision is to see the Body of Christ grow up into the measure of the stature of the fullness of the Lord Jesus Christ. Pastor Bynum and her husband, Bishop Paul E. Bynum, Sr. travel together and minister the Gospel of Jesus Christ in the Power of the Holy Spirit. They have two sons and four grandchildren.

About the Publisher

Let *Life to Legacy* bring your story to literary life! We offer the following publishing services: manuscript development, editing, transcription services, ghost-writing, cover design, copyright services, ISBN assignment, worldwide distribution, and eBook conversion.

We make the publishing process easy. Throughout production, we keep the author informed every step of the way. Even if you do not have a manuscript, that's not a problem for us. We can ghost-write your book from audio recordings or legible handwritten documents. Whether print-on-demand or trade publishing, we have packages to meet your publishing needs. At *Life to Legacy*, we take the stress out of becoming a published author.

Unlike other *so-called* publishers, we do more than just print books. Our books and eBooks are distributed to book buyers, distributors, and online retailers throughout the world – this is real publishing! Call us today for a free quote.

Please visit our website
www.Life2Legacy.com

or call us
877-267-7477

Send e-mail inquiries
Life2Legacybooks@att.net

www.ingramcontent.com/pod-product-compliance
Lightning Source LLC
Chambersburg PA
CBHW030940090426
42737CB00007B/487